Contents

EUROPEAN TRADE UNIONISM

Eric Jacobs

CROOM HELM LONDON

FIRST PUBLISHED 1973
© 1973 BY ERIC JACOBS

CROOM HELM LTD
2-10 ST JOHNS ROAD LONDON SW 11

HARDBACK ISBN 0-85664-091-3
PAPERBACK ISBN 0-85664-043-3

PRINTED AND BOUND IN GREAT BRITAIN
BY W & J MACKAY LIMITED, CHATHAM

TO BEVERLIE

Preface

This book has two aims. The first is to convey something of the undoubted differences between the trade union movements of Europe; the second is to indicate some of the equally undoubted similarities. European unions differ in their political and religious allegiances, their membership and structure, their success or failure. But they have much in common too, not least their problems.

All but the neutral countries of Europe had to face the agonies of reconstruction after the Second World War, and then the subtler pains of rapid economic growth. The first period was characterised by a high degree of amity in industrial relations; in the second period, industrial relations turned sour. It seemed, paradoxically, easier to distribute the meagre rations of the late 1940s than to divide the plenty of the late 1960s. The breakdown varied in its timing, its causes and its impact, but it happened everywhere, and it everywhere caught the unions, no matter what their ideology or style, as unprepared as it did managements or Government.

By the early 1970s a broad trend of reform had developed, some of it negotiated, some legislated. Reform was often awkwardly handled but the intention was much the same in every country; to refashion the institutions through which labour was represented to make them more efficient and effective, and to enhance workers' rights at every level, from the shopfloor to the boardroom to the national economy. And if there was no appreciable diminution in industrial unrest—far from it—it seemed possible to discern through the chaos the outlines of a new settlement for the last quarter of the century, suitable to a richer, more emancipated Europe, in which workers would no longer be willing to put up with the ancient hazards of unemployment, poor rewards, unsatisfying work or the arbitrary decisions of their employers, and in which employers would have to learn to accomodate themselves to that new fact.

1 *The Style of European Trade Unionism*

I recall two scenes. The first is in the office of a director of a once famous Clyde shipyard. It is a family firm and the director is a member of the family. The yard is in steep decline. Across the river is another yard which has just been rescued by a consortium of backers, underpinned by the government, from the bankruptcy towards which this one is heading. 'Do you realise that they've given the shop stewards a room to themselves?' the director splutters. 'And a telephone!' He is almost apoplectic with rage at this concession to the union enemy, at this break with the family tradition of constant, petty warfare with its own workforce.

The second scene is also set in offices, this time occupied by the employees' side of the works council at a steel products plant near Frankfurt. Although the council represents only some 4,000 workers, its offices are in a substantial block, suitable for the head-quarters of a medium-sized British union, or even of a national confederation of Italian unions. Its boardroom is not very much smaller than the one in which the General Council of Britain's Trades Union Congress (TUC) holds its regular monthly meetings, though it is shabbier. From one room comes a convivial sound, as of a party. I go in, am handed a glass of schnapps, then another, then a glass of beer. It is only four in the afternoon but it is, indeed, a party. The chairman of the council, a small, enthusiastic, slightly drunk man explains: 'You see, they are celebrating my birthday.'

These scenes prove nothing. The incidents are isolated and the situations in no way comparable (though as a matter of interest, the Clyde shipyard is now merged with its hated rival across the river, while the Frankfurt plant is still thriving on its own). But they have stayed in my mind because of what they suggest. The first is typical of the style of prickly, combative worker-manage-ment relationships, the second is far more relaxed. The Clyde speaks the rhetoric of class war: Frankfurt talks more amiably about partnership. On the Clyde, there is a sense of edginess, of unfinished business, of strife past and to come; while in Frankfurt it is not only the schnapps that induces calm—it is the confidence among works council members, the feeling they communicate that they have few problems they cannot work out quietly around a table with the employers.

These opposite styles say a good deal about the differences that divide European trade unionism. They are what I shall call the 'responsible' and the 'irresponsible' styles; the words being used in a purely descriptive sense, not to denote value. Most European trade unions operate in one style or the other, or at any rate along a scale that runs between the two. Their more obvious characteristics are these: 'responsible' trade unionists are confident of their place in society and secure in their role; 'irresponsible' trade unionists believe society is fundamentally hostile to their interests and barely willing to tolerate them. 'Responsible' trade unionists know they are powerful and use their power sparingly; 'irresponsible' trade unionists are less sure of their power and tend to use what they have much more often. 'Responsible' trade unionists seek to participate wherever decisions are made, in the boardrooms, in the ministries, in the major institutions of state, especially those that are concerned with economic planning and social security; 'irresponsible' trade unionists also want to influence the major decisions, but they are far more reluctant to abandon their strongholds in the streets and factories for a subtly compromising seat at a top table. 'Responsible' trade unionists generally, though not invariably, belong to a movement that is the overwhelmingly dominant power in their country; 'irresponsible' trade unionists tend to live in countries where the movement is fragmented.

Sweden and Germany provide the leading examples of 'responsible' trade unionism, France and Italy of the 'irresponsible'. Others lie somewhere in between. (The British TUC can never make up its mind which it is. It is, for example, desperately anxious to get round the table with the government on economic questions. From time to time it succeeds, but it somehow never manages to stay seated for long.)

There are some indicators that tend immediately to confirm the distinction between the two types. One good guide to 'responsibility' is the attitude of union movements towards the idea of putting workers' representatives on company boards. According to a survey carried out in 1972 among non-communist and non-denominational movements, British, Italian, French and Belgian unions opposed workers sitting on boards, while German, Scandinavian and Dutch unions were in favour. This is what one would expect. But there is no need, at this stage, to look for proofs. The distinction is not meant to be definitive; only to convey a first impression of different kinds of trade union.

On this basis, the difference between the two types is detectable almost on sight. German and Swedish trade unions really do look as if they are equal partners with the employers. The headquarters of the Deutsche Gewerkschaftsbund (DGB) in Dusseldorf are indistinguishable from the office blocks of the international corporations like Philips that surround it, and so are the headquarters of a DGB member union like IG Metall in Frankfurt. In contrast, French and Italian unions tend to operate from premises in old private houses or seedy office buildings that have seen better days. The Swedish trade union movement owns the biggest circulation daily paper in Stockholm and the DGB the fourth largest bank in Germany. French and Italian union resources are manifestly slender. Contributions are small and few people believe that, small as they are, they are paid regularly by the number of people the unions claim as members.

One useful way of picking up clues about the differences between movements is to listen to what they say about themselves in statements and programmes setting out their aims and ambitions, and in controversy.

Here is one French trade union centre, the Confédération Générale du Travail (CGT), describing in its propaganda material the lot of the working man and the role of the union in trying to do something about it:

In their daily life, workers are at grips with the incessant bludgeonings of capital, the consequences of the exploitation which they undergo and the multiple attempts of the employers and the state to aggravate it.

They have to repel constant attacks against their standard of life, to defend the purchasing power of their wages against rising prices, to fight to improve it. They come up against refusal to meet the claims that present conditions of life and work make pressing, such as those for the reduction of working hours, bringing forward the age of retirement and better pensions.

They have to defend themselves against unemployment and job insecurity, to preserve and enlarge their union liberties.

Making claims is a continuous fight. It requires mass union struggles in various but vigorous forms, on a scale which will translate the discontent of the workers, their will to defend their interests, and permit them to do so with success.

That is one voice. Here is another, the DGB's:

The self-evident endeavour of the German trade unions to consider demands in the consciousness of their responsibility for the economy and society as a whole has been concretely demonstrated by the policy they have pursued during the last twenty years.

Proof is provided, in the first place, by the extensive and indisputable efforts of the trade unions in the field of education and training. Not only technical skills have been taught; over and above such teaching their endeavour has been, by providing him with all relevant information, and by sharpening his powers of perception, to educate the working man to be a citizen conscious of his responsibilities within a free order of society. This endeavour will render comprehensible the constant vigilance of the trade unions aimed at preventing infiltration by totalitarian elements. Part of this endeavour is also the participation of the trade unions in the great social and political problems affecting our nation.

Moreover, in the field of free collective bargaining, the German trade unions have, since 1945, demonstrated the responsibility of their policy, the aim of which has at all times been to promote the reconstruction of the economy. The Council of Economic Experts and the Federal Bank, as impartial bodies, have both paid tribute to this fact. Strikes have been extremely rare, and have been conducted only in the last resort, for the settlement of disputes.

The trade union attitude towards the state has long been an affirmative one. The unions are represented on a great variety of bodies within the administration, in order effectively to represent and safeguard the interests of the workers. The same principle applies to the degree of influence exercised by the workpeople and their trade unions at establishment level.[1]

The contrast could hardly be more complete. The CGT, it seems, lives in a wholly hostile world. The employers are against them, joined by the state in a conspiracy to cut workers' living standards where they can, and certainly to resist all attempts at improving them. Strikes are legitimate, necessary, even desirable —a way of life. For the DGB, on the other hand, Germany is friendly soil. It goes out of its way to identify itself as a responsible component of the nation, anxious to play its part, in sympathy with the broad aims of the constitution, vigilant against its subversion. It dislikes strikes and it is eager to underline how few of them it has had.

Here are two other voices. The first is that of the Swedish Trade Union Confederation (LO), describing and justifying the Basic Agreement it drew up with the employers in 1938, which, with modifications, has survived ever since as the foundation of industrial relations:

It cannot be emphasised too strongly that the first and foremost problem facing the trade unions in their activities is how to exercise their freedom in a way that is compatible with responsibility towards society. This involves rather more than the simple issue of whether these obligations should be self-imposed or placed upon the unions by the legislature. To accept responsibility voluntarily is to give practical evidence of maturity; to have refused would have been to demonstrate basic inability to manage one's own affairs.[2]

The second is a description, provided by Italian trade unionists, of the way in which their regular wage negotiations in the rubber industry are conducted:

> The negotiations for the renewal of the national agreement begin before the old one has expired—on the unions' initiative—and they are *always* [my italics] accompanied by industrial action to encourage the employer to take into account the full scope of the workers' claims, which otherwise they seem to find difficult.[3]

Again, the contrast is clear. For the Swedish trade unionists, like the Germans, maturity and a sense of obligation towards society are a matter of pride. For the Italians, the first step in an argument is a strike. Struggle is a way of life; as much a virtue to them as it is to the French.

Contradictory these voices may be, but they are confident enough of what they are saying; each is sure it is right. But not all union movements are so certain. There are quavering notes in the chorus, the sound of those who do not quite know where they stand or exactly what it is they stand for. These are some reflections on the future of trade unionism by Jean Kulakowski, secretary of the European Organisation of the World Council of Labour (WCL):

> We consider, with some others, that from a movement of proletarian revolt, through the present vicissitudes of a movement obsessed by its heroic past, partially settled in a consumption civilisation and marked down by the danger of technocracy, the trade unionism must open on a conception of a free man in an organised society. At this price only it will avoid the disaffection of the working people and the stagnation and it will be the leaven of the world of tomorrow. [It is not only the English that is fractured here, though, perhaps unfairly, I have left it in the translation provided by the

WCL's Brussels' office.]

It is especially worth listening to what unions have to say about themselves when they are in the process of changing. All unions change—as all institutions must if they are to stay alive—but they do not all discuss it out loud. It is highly characteristic of 'responsible' trade unions that they should be seen to make changes deliberately while the 'irresponsible' prefer not to tamper with their original programmes, even if they no longer bear much relation to reality. The points about retirement and pensions would only have to be edited out to make the CGT statement as pertinent to 1871 as to May 1971, when it was published. In CGT ideology, it seems, nothing much has happened in a hundred years.

Here, on the other hand, is the President of the Swedish LO thinking his way towards a shift in the direction of union policy that has now taken place.

> Many people are wondering whether the time has not come for the trade union movement to take the plunge into the management pool—to take on management functions and set itself on an equal footing with the capital owner in the direction of the affairs of the undertaking.
>
> We have always been cautious in these matters, believing that to be able to assert ourselves both at work and in society at large, the trade union movement needed not only to be strong, but also free and independent. . . .
>
> The most discussed means of trade union participation in management is representation on a company's board of directors. Although this idea has in the past had a rather luke-warm response from the trade union movement, in the long run it becomes increasingly clear that a practice whereby workpeople and their representatives are excluded from the most important decision-making bodies in the firm, is un-satisfactory. We shall probably therefore finally opt for a formal system of workers' representation on the board.[4]

The DGB has revised its programme perhaps more fully than any other movement in recent years. When it formulated its first set of objectives in 1949, it inherited a good deal of the philosophy of its pre-Nazi ancestor, the German Free Trade Unions. It was committed to economic planning and widespread nationalisation. One historian of the movement describes it as 'virtually socialist revolutionary'.[5] But at Dusseldorf in 1963 it adopted a new programme. The emphasis was radically altered. Planning was no longer seen as a centralised, dirigiste affair, but rather as a more skilful and co-ordinated deployment of conventional economic management techniques. There should be public influence on private investment, the programme said, 'without depriving individual enterprises of the final decision as to the nature and extent of their investments'.[6]

The DGB declared an aim with which no trade unionist could quarrel: 'to bring about a fundamental reform of the economy and of society, the object of which is to ensure that each and every citizen shall be enabled to participate on a basis of equality in every economic, political and cultural decision affecting his nation.'[6] But this was not to be achieved by the traditional method of seizing the commanding heights of the economy. The broad lines of Germany's market economy were accepted. Instead, the emancipation of the worker was to be won by an increase in his influence at the point where, within the system, it was now seen to be crucial—at the level of the company and the plant. There was full employment and steady growth, and it seemed that both could henceforth be taken for granted. What was now seen to be important were more local and more intimate decisions than those that preoccupied an older generation of the movement, such things as investment, promotion, hiring and firing, the pace of work, the introduction of new production techniques, and so on. It was these matters, the DGB decided, that the worker should now be concerned about and it put a new emphasis on an old, but in the past less compelling, concept—that of 'co-determination'. The DGB has adopted a motto: 'as much competition as possible; as much planning as necessary'. It is a typically equable phrase—cautious, pragmatic, open-minded.

From the examples quoted so far, it might be thought that all union controversy and all differences were between European countries. And there would be a certain limited justification for this. In a country where trade unionism is weak, all trade unions are likely to share in the weakness; some characteristics are undoubtedly national. But not all. On the contrary, by no means does every trade union in the same country speak with the same voice.

In March 1972, a young militant maoist, René-Pierre Overney, was shot dead by a security officer in an incident at the gates of the Renault factory at Billancourt. There followed, according to *Le Monde*, 'a war of declarations and communiqués of great vivacity':

> M. Edmond Maire [secretary of the Confédération Francaise Démocratique du Travail (CFDT)] had opened fire by reproaching the 'militant communists' of the CGT for having taken from the start of the affair 'an attitude not of union leadership, but of political leadership'. The confederate office of the CGT replied to this 'intolerable interference in the internal affairs of the CGT' by stressing that 'only the employers, the authorities and those who create divisions in their service' would be able 'to congratulate' M. Maire.
>
> The CFDT came back soon to the charge, accusing the CGT of 'searching deliberately for an incident in order to hide the difficulties that it meets among workers and public opinion as a result of the positions it has taken up following the death of Pierre Overney'.[7]

However, as *Le Monde* noted, the two organisations were careful to avoid a total breach. They finished their polemic by reassuring each other that they had no intention of letting their verbal differences interfere with their common front on practical matters. In wage negotiations in the nationalised industries, for one, they intended to stick together.

As the outcome of that argument suggests, there are limits to the significance of words alone. Style and rhetoric can be revealing, but they can also be deceptive. The TUC still demands in its constitution the nationalisation of the railways, even though the railways have in fact been nationalised for twenty-five years; and the desire of the DGB for fundamental reform of society, just

quoted, would fit easily enough into the preamble to the constitution of any left or right-wing union movement and actually
sounds most out of place in the DGB's own prosaic programme.

Exactly how deceptive words can be was brought home to me
by a phrase in a conversation not long ago with Pierre Cerniti, the
young leader of FIM, one of the Italian metalworkers' unions. He
said that it was wrong to pay workers in dispute out of a strike
fund because only 'true sacrifice raises political consciousness'. It
had a fine militant-marxist ring, but should it be taken literally?
Or did the phrase merely disguise the fact that the FIM, like most
Italian unions, had no strike funds? And could that, in turn,
explain why Italian union action takes the form it does—the
one-day strike, the half-day strike, the one-hour strike, the half-
hour strike, the 'hiccup' strike, the 'chequer-board' strike—almost
anything but an all-out confrontation? What at first sight appears
to be a brave declaration may soon turn out to be something else.
The facts dictate the words and not the other way about.

It is the same with the other examples of union style that have
been mentioned in this chapter. The differences are deeper than
eccentricity or local quirk. They all have causes, or at least a
background. The contrast between war on the Clyde and peace
in Frankfurt clearly has something to do with Scotland's four
decades of heavy unemployment and Germany's two decades of
the opposite. And the multiple trade unionism of a British shipyard creates difficulties that the single trade union in the Frankfurt
plant avoids.

But explanation cannot stop here. For one thing, there is more
than one kind of multiple trade unionism. In Britain, the half-
dozen unions in a shipyard exist to represent different grades of
worker; they are craft unions that have emerged from the technical
and social history of their industry. In the rest of Europe, on the
other hand, most trade unionism is on an individual industry basis.
All shipyard workers are grouped together. Where they split is
over their ideologies. It is not because CGT members do different
jobs from DGB members that their unions seem so unalike—nor
even because one is French and the other German. It is because the
CGT, though it claims to be independent is predominantly com-

munist, and the DGB, though it also claims to be independent is predominantly social democratic.

Differences in Europe are further complicated by trade unionism founded on religion, and more complicated still when the religious content is weakened and the movement is left with—with what? With the kind of obscure vision represented by the WCL musings on the future I have quoted. Hence, too, the acrimonious dispute between the communist CGT and the formerly Christian CFDT—very French in manner, but also very typical of the controversies that can crop up between a marxist union movement of a traditional type and a movement that has been uprooted from its religious traditions and is shifting uncertainly towards its own brand of militant socialism; a union, bluntly, without a clear industrial or ideological identity.

Fragmented trade unionism may also help to explain the relative strengths and weaknesses of the movement in different countries. The need to choose between ideologies in France and Italy appears to have kept union membership low, while the broad unanimity of the Swedish and German movements must be among the reasons why they attract a larger following. And yet fragmented unionism can also be numerically strong, as it is in Britain and Belgium.

If anything is clear by now, it must be the fact that the make-up of European trade unionism is extremely complicated. In each country unions obviously discharge something of the same function, representing workers for the purpose of regulating relations with employers and with society as a whole. But, equally obviously, the form this representation takes varies widely. Why? Because the special character of each union movement is intimately involved with the country in which it has developed—its political, economic and social history. It is to these factors that we must now turn.

Notes

1. *Co-determination: A Contemporary Demand*, DGB, Dusseldorf, 1966, p. 11.

2. *Development of Labour Peace in Sweden*, LO, Stockholm, 1971, pp. 23–24.

3. Statement by Pirelli-Dunlop shop stewards' international steering committee, February 1972.

4 *Industrial Democracy*, Arne Geijer, LO, Stockholm, 1971, p. 5.

5 *The History of the German Labour Movement*, Helga Grebing, Oswald Wolff, London, 1969, p. 175.

6. DGB, *op. cit.*, p. 10.

7. *Le Monde*, 9 March 1972.

2 Ideology, Politics and Religion

In order to enter the Paris office of the French employers' organisation—the *Patronat* as it is called—you have to undergo a strange procedure, rather like the complicated manoeuvrings needed to get into a submarine under water. You press the door-bell. In due course, the catch is silently released on a heavily reinforced iron gate. Once through it the gate closes behind you. Next you must satisfy the guardian of the entrance, who lurks behind thick glass and can only be communicated with by microphone. When he is convinced that you are a *bona fide* visitor, he releases the catch on a second, equally impressive iron gate, and you're inside. You may have to wait, trapped between the two gates, while someone else is allowed out for both are never open at the same time. Those on the inside, it seems, do not entirely trust the world beyond.

The gates are perhaps more symbolic than real—a determined mob would not find them too difficult to break down—but they symbolise something that is very real indeed—a pattern of industrial conflict that is sharp and occasionally near-revolutionary, fully reflecting the violent upheavals of France's social and political history. For if France's political development has seemed to evolve through a series of major crises, so has its industrial relations. It is typical that advances in trade union rights, which in other countries have been secured gradually through negotiated trial and error backed by cautious parliamentary support, should in France have been won only by street fighting and factory occupation and other forms of extremism, for example in 1936 and again in 1968.

There is, of course, in every country where it has taken root, a close tie between trade unions and politics. As trade unions emerged in the wake of industrialisation and the creation of an urban working class, at different times in different European countries, their leaders have had to enlist political support simply in order to survive the initial suspicion and, usually, hostility of the ruling regimes. Furthermore, trade unions sprung from ambitions for a better life for working men and women that could never have been fulfilled only by negotiations with employers about wages and conditions of work. The first signs of trade unionism were in the formation of small societies to protect a number of the welfare and other social interests of groups of workers, and the representation of such interests remains the most enduring function of trade unionism. But the radical social changes, and the wholesale dislocation of existing patterns of rural life and work that industrialisation brought, generated many different demands for yet more social changes to soften the impact on the new working classes—some mild and gradual, some revolutionary, most with at least a touch of Utopia about them. In its early days, trade unionism was just as much about politics as purely industrial affairs, and the association of the unions with politics has survived.

The present pattern of continental European trade unionism is heavily marked by political events in ways that differ strongly from the experience of, say, Britain, the United States or Australia. In these three countries, a comparatively peaceful domestic political history since industrialisation began has encouraged the development of formidable jungles of autonomous trade unions designed to represent the interests of particular groups of workers, based on types of skill, or on industries or on a combination of both. Once organised on this narrow and haphazard basis they have come together in loose national federations to deal centrally with problems of importance to every union. These federations discuss with government and business organisations all kinds of problems of social and economic policy—employment, safety, the law, welfare, prices and incomes policies—while member unions retain virtually complete independence to do their own negotiations with their own employers. In union movements of this kind, members hold widely different views on politics and religion; they can and do quarrel violently. The union or the whole movement may swing from one extreme to another in politics. But Catholic and communist belong to the same union and the union stays affiliated to the same national centre, though there are strains and sometimes expulsions, because it is the only central union organisation the country has, or the only one worth joining. The interests of the working group and the union come first. Politics and religion, the broader ideological questions, take second place to these interests.

In much of Europe, on the other hand, the emphasis is very much the other way round. A worker in, for instance, a Renault car plant in France is not faced with the choice of becoming a member of one of a dozen or more competing unions, each representing distinct groups or grades of worker, as he would be in a car plant in England (or with no choice of unions at all, as in America). Instead, the French worker would choose between unions that each claim to represent the same grades, but from a different ideological standpoint. For him, the choice would not be between a union for skilled craftsmen and one for unskilled labourers, but between unions that are in origin either communist, Catholic or socialist. In this kind of union movement, political interests come first. Political interest groups created the unions, not the unions the political interest groups. A turbulent political history since industrialisation has encouraged the growth of a union movement divided along strictly ideological lines. The precise mixture varies from country to country in Europe, but the echo of ancient disputes between the religious and the secular, the revolutionary and the constitutionalist, can still be heard in most of them.

Take the case of Luxembourg. It is a small country whose total population of 340,000, let alone its employed population of 150,000, is smaller than the membership of a good many British or American trade unions. And yet a recent note on the Luxembourg trade union movement could say that it was 'essentially characterised by its pluralism and by its diversity'.[1] Organised workers today number only some 50,000. But there are three national union centres to cater for them, and until 1966 when the communists merged with the socialists, there were four. The three organisations that survive are the 29,000-member socialist CGT, the 11,000 strong Christian LCGB and the FEP with 10,000, a non-political grouping of white-collar workers.

The CGT talks the language of socialism everywhere. It declares: 'the trade union movement repudiates false values, such as rights claimed on grounds of birth or wealth, and will carry on the struggle against the oligarchy of the banks and the monopolies which has made itself the master of the means of production.

'The trade union movement wants to make the wage-earner, now forced to sell his labour, a free participant in the common task of production.'

The Christian LCGB, on the other hand, repudiates socialist ideas of class struggle and opposes nationalisation. It does not want to overthrow the established order, whether economic or political. It seeks improvements in the workers' social and economic conditions by, for instance, guaranteed full employment.

The thinking of the CGT owes much to Marx; that of the LCGB to successive papal encyclicals.

To account for the precise pattern of ideologies in the trade union movements of every country of Europe would mean re-telling almost the whole modern history of each country, from the Reformation onwards. This is not the place to attempt such a task. But the ingredients in the common mixture can be seen clearly enough by looking briefly at the development of trade unionism in a single country—Germany.

In Germany, as in most countries, labour organisations were at the start shaky, uncertain and divided. But in 1848, when legal restrictions were lifted for the first time, the first of a number of continuing sources of dispute came into the open—the argument between revolution and reform. As it did elsewhere, shadowy prototypes of trade unionism emerged in Germany with the beginnings of industrialisation at the start of the century—benefit funds, educational associations and the like. The fact that many journeymen had to travel to find work combined with political oppression in Germany itself led to the founding of more ambitious organisations in secret abroad. One of these was the League of the Just, which became the Communist League in London in 1847. Under the influence of Marx and Engels its aims were clearly revolutionary—'the overthrow of the bourgeoisie, the rule of the proletariat . . . the creation of a new society without classes and privileges'.

The first Communist League was dissolved in 1848, and in the same year another short-lived organisation was founded with quite different views. This was the General German Workers' Fraternisation. Under the influence of Stephan Born, its objects were strictly limited, pragmatic and gradual: a parliamentary democracy with a system of universal suffrage, the right to form trade unions, the establishment of labour exchanges, a health service and insurance benefits.

'Moreover—and it is well that our brothers, the workers, know it—we condemn rioting and we protest against every kind of disorder. We are not plotting against the existing government, we only want to be given a place in our common fatherland.'[2]

Thus, from the very beginning, the two themes of revolution and reform were clearly stated. And in workers' organisations, politics and ideology were to continue for a long time to predominate over narrow industrial objectives.

In 1863, the German General Workers' Association was founded in Leipzig by Ferdinand Lasalle, and in 1869, the Social Democratic Workers' Party was founded in Eisenach by Wilhelm Liebknecht and August Babel. Both were primarily political organisations, though they set up trade union wings to their movements, and they were in broad agreement in their social and economic programmes. It was on the question of German unity that they differed. Lasalle favoured Prussia and the federation of the German states; the others opposed Prussia and favoured complete unification of Germany.

This primarily political colour does not seem to have helped the cause of conventional trade unionism. When, for example, the Lasalleans formed a General Union of German Workers in 1869, Lasalle intended them to be an arm of the political organisation rather than an industrial movement. They were unable to agree on how the unions should be organised—whether they should be centralised or local, or whether they should be subordinated to the political party or left to represent workers' interests. As a result, they became fragmented and, under various pressures, were dissolved five years later.

Nor, of course, did the movements' political militancy do any-thing to endear them to the conservative government. So the two socialist parties, which had merged in 1875 were disbanded in 1878 following the passage of the Anti-Socialist law. Virtually all their activities, including trade unionism, had to cease, though the parliamentary group was allowed to continue. Only the liberal-professional Hirsch-Duncker associations, which were founded in 1868, were allowed to operate openly and their members had to give undertakings that they neither belonged to nor supported the Socialist Party. For the rest, trade unions were obliged to take on a twilight existence and operate as benefit clubs or something that was equally harmless in the eye of authority.

It was not until 1890, when the Anti-Socialist Law was finally repealed, that the unions began to emerge again, and this time fully in their own right. In the meantime there were several parallel developments. New types of trade unionism appeared and the Government introduced some measures of social reform. And these responses were undoubtedly to some extent shaped by the political and sectarian character of the early labour movements.

The first development was the beginning of Christian trade unionism. Although Catholic workers' associations were started in the middle of the century the Catholic trade union movement in Germany is generally agreed to date from a speech made by Wilhelm Ketteler, Bishop of Mainz, in 1869, which indicated a new approach to social questions by the Church. For the first time the hierarchy was seen to give its support for higher wages and shorter hours for workers, and for laws to protect working women and children. The trend towards Catholic concern for the human effects of industrialisation was accelerated throughout Europe by the papal encyclical *Rerum Novarum* in 1891. Protestant workers' associations were also founded, from 1882 onwards. In 1899 both denominations were linked, in spite of some opposition from among Catholics, in a Confederation of Christian Unions. By the First World War, this confederation was around 350,000 strong.

The second development was the foundation in 1868 of the Hirsch-Duncker associations. This was an attempt by the German Progressive Party (liberals) to create a counterweight to the socialist organisations. Instead of destroying capitalist society, their aim was to improve workers' conditions within it. Liberal trade unionism as such scarcely survives in Europe today, except in Belgium, but the Hirsch-Duncker associations illustrate the origins of a kind of trade unionism that still flourishes in one form or another in most countries in Europe—professional organisations representing white-collar interests, often teachers or civil servants.

There was, at the same time, a third development in response to workers' agitation. While Bismarck's government outlawed socialist organisations, it made some efforts to remove the sources of discontent that bred them. A series of insurance laws (national health, 1883; accident, 1884; old age and disablement, 1889) were introduced. They may have been seen by the socialists as merely tactical—an attempt to buy off groups who would otherwise seek more thoroughgoing reforms of society—but they were also the first real steps towards comprehensive social welfare in any industrialised country and they still remain the foundations of German social security.

With the dropping of the ban on socialist organisations, a General Committee of German Trade Unions was formed in November 1890. It had political aims and a clear socialist ideology, but there was now a definite and acknowledged distinction between the functions of the political and the trade union wings of the movement.

'The difference between the political activity carried on by the Workers' Party and the tasks of the unions rests on the fact that the former seeks to transform the organisation of existing society, while the efforts of the latter, being circumscribed by law, are anchored in present-day bourgeois society.'[3]

Now that the break had been made, the trade unionists began to turn the tables on the politicians. The 'Free' trade unions, as they came to be called, could no longer be thought of as the poor relations of left-wing politics. On the contrary, the unions' incomes far exceeded that of the party by the time of the First World War and by then, too, union officials accounted for almost a third of the socialist seats in Parliament. At the same time, the unions were strengthening their influence in other ways, by supporting or founding consumer co-operatives, housing associations and insurance companies. The realities of the situation were finally recognised at the Socialist Party (SPD) Congress of 1906 when the unions and the party were declared to be of equal importance to one another. Organisationally, the unions were moving towards the type of structure that is now common in Europe. Although they originally tended to recruit the more skilled men in industry, the craftsmen, as they increased their penetration of the working population so they moved towards the idea of one union for each industry by means of mergers and amalgamations, a strategy that was far advanced by 1914.

By then, indeed, the trade union arm of the labour movement was rather more interested in making deals than in making revolutions, in chalking up solid, identifiable advances for their members than in overthrowing bourgeois society. In 1913, the trade unions concluded some 13,500 pay-rate agreements covering more than two million workers. So far as unions were concerned the reformist and not the revolutionary road had been adopted. The trade union leaders were content to leave the overthrow and the remaking of society to their allies in the SPD.

The First World War brought radical changes in Germany as it did in the rest of Europe. In the rush of militarist euphoria that swept the country, in which the international ideals of the socialist movement were completely smothered, the unions agreed to bury their differences with the employers for the duration of the fighting. In return they were granted new recognition by both employers and government, a new status of equality with employers' organisations and new rights to recruit and organise their memberships.

In the revolutionary chaos of the war's end, the unions made several new advances. In 1918, when socialists were for the first time in government, they achieved a new concordat with the employers, gaining more freedom to organise and providing for the cherished eight-hour day (though in practice extensive overtime was to make nonsense of the apparent reduction in working hours). In 1920, under the new Weimar Republic, a Works Council

Law was passed, establishing voluntary elected councils in small enterprises and compulsory councils in firms with more than twenty employees. Council members could look at company books and had a vote on the board of directors. In three industries a form of joint worker-owner management was introduced—in potash, coal and steel—though in steel it was soon abolished and in the others the experiment was not a great success (unions and management made deals with each other at the expense of the public and the government had to step in).

In the pre-Nazi period, the unions continued to expand. Membership reached a peak of nearly five million. By the end of the 1920s collective agreements covered over twelve million workers. In one Parliament, more than one-third of socialist MPs were trade unionists.

The trade unions were now far from revolutionary. They were concerned to preserve and develop the gains they had won under parliamentary democracy, and the preservation of parliamentary democracy was perhaps their principle political aim. They hunted out and expelled revolutionary communists, forcing them to try, unsuccessfully, to set up their own rival union organisations. Union leaders acquiesced in the Works Council Law though they did not like it, fearing with a good deal of justice that the councils would undermine their own influence; but from their point of view it was at least better than having to put up with workers' committees on the Soviet model, emblems of the bolshevism they hated.

The Second World War and its Cold War aftermath had a traumatic effect on labour movements all over Europe, and in Germany its consequences were multiplied by the experiences of Nazism and the division of the country after 1945. Hitler, of course, eliminated the trade unions as soon as he had seized power in 1933 and for twelve years workers had been organised in, or rather compelled to join, a Labour Front, which was nothing more than a coercive arm of the Nazi Party. As soon as the war ended, however, the unions began to re-emerge and in a very real sense it was the workers and their organisations that started on the reconstruction of the country. But they quickly came up against new problems. The political wing of the movement was rapidly absorbed into the Communist Party in East Germany and the unions in the Western sectors were unable to join up with those in the East.

Nazism and Communism between them confirmed the West German labour movement in its faith in the virtues of solidarity and parliamentary democracy and brought a new distaste for ideological schism. Even the Catholics fell into line. Although the Church had created a union movement that mustered over a million members in the 1920s, the Catholic Workers' Associations that were revived after the war firmly supported the idea of a single national union centre, the DGB. (A Catholic union centre was established again in 1955, under the influence of the international Catholic union movement, but it has never managed to raise a significant union membership.) One of the very few major groups to remain outside the DGB is the DAG, a half-million-strong union of white-collar workers, and it was excluded not on ideological but on structural grounds. In 1948, the DGB opted for a system of vertical industrial trade unionism, and the DAG was unacceptable because it organised horizontally, among staff doing the same work but in different industries.

Since the war, the unions and the political party—the DGB and the SPD—have continued to march, if not in step, at any rate in reasonable harmony. While both at first adopted programmes of a more or less traditional type of radical socialism, both revised their programmes completely in the light of the success of the 'social market' economy and developed far more flexible policies, the SPD in 1959 and the DGB four years later. But the separation of the two was now complete. Though there is no doubt that the sympathies of the majority of DGB leaders lie with the SPD, the DGB now supplies a substantial number of MPs not only to that party but to the opposition Christian Democrats as well; and one of the DGB vice-presidents is now regularly elected from the Christian Democrats.

The German story contains most of the themes and incidents of the European labour movement as a whole. The onset of industrialisation was not matched by changes in the political structure of society. Early attempts to organise workers were confused and divided in their aims, and oppression was the usual response of the authorities. In consequence, organised workers, while forming rudimentary trade and welfare organisations which were generally restricted and local, tended first to be organised for political rather than purely industrial purposes—to confront the state as much as the employers. Solutions to the problems of the new class of wage earners and alleviation of their distress were sought in prescriptions for repairing the whole fabric of society, not just by stitching up the tears here and there. Ideology preceded organisation and political and religious movements created trade unions in their own image. Revolution, reaction and, especially, war enforced rapid change. The result has been to bequeath a patchwork quilt of union movements to modern Europe.

Most countries show something of each traditional strain in their corner of the patchwork—Christian, communist, social democratic and independent—though the blend varies widely. The Scandinavian countries, for example, are hardly affected by religious trade unionism, while in the Netherlands and Belgium it predominates (though in Ireland, where today religious sectarianism is more alive than elsewhere in Europe, the unions are not formally affected since they were modelled essentially on the British pattern in which the interests of the working group are placed before any ideology). The independent unions, too, are very mixed. Though they usually recruit white-collar workers—often teachers or civil servants—there are other kinds as well, like the eighteen separate organisations that represent different groups of workers on the Paris Metro, or the tiny movement in Sweden originating from the now largely forgotten anarcho-syndicalist theories that were popular in the early years of this century.

In the period immediately after the Second World War it looked as if these differences would dwindle into insignificance, or even disappear altogether. For the sense of unity and solidarity that was to be such a powerful shaping force in the German movement affected other countries in Western Europe that had been liberated from Nazi rule.

In the Netherlands, for example, leaders of Christian and

socialist unions met secretly during the war and determined a set of formal rules for co-operation between unions nationally and locally; among other things, they agreed to ask for uniform rates of subscription from all their members so as to avoid competition between them—so that on 5 May 1945, the day of final liberation, a joint Council of Trade Union Centres was already in existence and able to make its public bow.

The same sort of thing happened in France and Italy. In Italy the *Patto di Roma* (Rome Pact) of 3 June 1944, created the General Italian Confederation of Labour (CGIL) to replace the Fascist unions with a new movement that would take in all the pre-Fascist tendencies.

But it was not long before the old ideological divisions re-appeared. Even in the Netherlands the unity forged under wartime occupation was dissolved. In a pastoral letter of 1954 the Dutch bishops forbade Catholics to join socialist unions, and in response the socialist NVV withdrew from the Council of Trade Union Centres. (Secret talks between the bishops and the NVV led to a resumption of co-operation between the different union centres, but only at the level of the most senior leadership. The Catholic proscription on membership of socialist unions was not lifted until 1966.)

The more characteristic breakdown was, however, over politics. The early postwar unity between the unions in France and Italy was sustained by unity in government, in both cases formed by broad coalitions. But the governments of de Gaulle and de Gasperi were soon dissolved—partly under Cold War pressures—and co-operation between trade unionists disappeared with them. The complexities of French and Italian electoral politics became mirrored in those of the trade union movement. In Italy, the communists had dominated the original joint federation, the CGIL. In June 1948 an alliance was formed by Christian, social democratic and republican trade unionists which four months later was turned into a new confederation, the LCGIL. The following year, however, the social democrats and the republicans with-drew to form their own federation. Some returned a year later to rejoin the Christians in a new confederation, the CISL, while others joined a rump of socialists, who had never liked the LCGIL, to form a new organisation, UIL. For most of the postwar period the communist, social democratic and Christian divisions have flourished as before.

At the international level the ideological divisions reflect those of the individual countries. The mood of reconciliation that followed the end of the war in Europe led at first to the foundation of a single organisation linking the major national movements, including those of East and West, but it split apart in the late 1940s. The communists established an International in Prague, the World Federation of Trade Unions (WFTU), and the non-communists set up their own world organisation in Brussels, the International Confederation of Free Trade Unions (ICFTU).

The resulting tangle of Internationals was neatly demonstrated in a paragraph in the 1972 report to the 10th Congress of the ICFTU, in which the Christian International, the World Council of Labour (WCL), is taken to task for its attitude towards the Communists:

> Following the contacts which have been established between the WCL and the WFTU, the former has been at pains to stress that it would like to strengthen its relations with the ICFTU, without severing its relations with the WFTU. We have insisted that it is impossible for the ICFTU to co-operate with the WFTU, in view of the fact that the ideological gap between the two organisations cannot be bridged, and have stressed that future relations with the WCL would depend on the nature and type of WCL relations with the WFTU.[4]

It is a peculiar irony that an organisation like the ICFTU which groups together union movements with a strong marxist tradition like the German DGB, should fall out with a body like the WCL, whose traditions are stoutly anti-marxist, because the WCL is getting too close to the communist WFTU for their comfort.

The existence of rival internationals severely inhibits the already difficult business of co-ordinating trade union activity across national borders, especially in relation to the multi-national companies. International union action of this kind is generally conducted through trade secretariats, most of them based in Geneva, which link up unions with interests in the same industries, such as chemicals or engineering, all over the world. But the secretariats themselves tend to be either linked to the ICFTU directly or hostile to the WFTU-oriented unions, and thus unable to include communist trade unions. This can often make formal international co-operation impossible since workers in, say, the German motor industry are likely to find the most powerful organisations of their counterparts in France or Italy to be communist and therefore excluded from the relevant secretariat in Geneva. When British and Italian workers wanted to act together over the redundancies that followed the merger between Dunlop and Pirelli they were unable to do so officially. The main British unions with members at Dunlop are affiliated to the International Chemical Workers' Federation, while the main Italian union was not. So in Britain the initiative in calling a one-day strike in 1972 was taken unofficially by a shop stewards' committee that had made its own private contacts in Italy, while at Pirelli the unions themselves officially backed the strike. There was simply no way in which the leaders of the unions in both countries could get together formally to discuss the problems that affected them both.

There are, however, some signs that the ideological struggles within the union movements of Europe, both nationally and internationally, may be weakening. After the 'hot autumn' of industrial action that enveloped Italy in 1969, the country's three national union centres came under strong pressure from below to forget their political differences and unite. Some workers joined all three as a gesture of protest and others told their employers to deduct union dues from their pay packets—and then deliberately neglected to say which union should get the money. A programme for fusion was drawn up and agreed—one of the main stumbling blocks was the insistence that union officials should no longer hold political office but choose one career or the other, to which the communists were most reluctant to agree—but political pressures were revived by the election campaign of 1972 and the programme had to be modified.

Denominational rigidity has also weakened. In France, the Confédération Francaise des Travailleurs Chrétiens began to loosen its ties with the Church as early as 1946, when mention of papal encyclicals was removed from its statutes and replaced by a broad reference to Christian social morality. It also drew away from the Christian Democrats (MRP) in politics and in 1964 it eliminated the word 'Christian' from its title and substituted 'Democratic'. It is now unambiguously socialist, but that no longer makes it out of place in its International, the former International Confederation of Christian Trade Unions, which in 1968 also shed Christianity from its name and became the thoroughly secular World Council of Labour. In the Netherlands, too, a programme has been drawn up for uniting the Catholic and socialist union movements, though the Protestants have decided to remain independent.

It may be that the dissolution of ideologically divided trade unionism will get its most powerful impetus from events in Brussels or Geneva rather than from within the movements of individual European countries. Britain's entry into the EEC will bring the largest union confederation in Europe, the TUC, firmly on to the Continental stage. British union leaders have made it clear that they want communist and Christian confederations brought into contact with the new organisation that has been created to represent the unions of the nine EEC countries in European affairs, instead of there being, as now, three separate channels of consultation with the EEC institutions—communist, 'Christian' and social democratic. It remains to be seen how successful the British initiative will be, but it is unlikely that an organisation as large as the TUC will be without influence. And if international differences are reduced, national divisions could go the same way. One of the main obstacles to the success of the Italian reunification scheme was precisely the reluctance of the three union centres to drop their different international affiliations.

Today, indeed, the divisions between union movements look increasingly irrelevant, historical survivals sustained by bureaucratic inertia rather than differences that match real needs. To some extent, though, it can be seen to fulfil a function as a kind of substitute for conventional politics. Ideologically divided trade unionism appears to thrive best in countries where parliamentary democracy is limited or frustrated—either by the complexities of coalition government, as in Italy or the Netherlands or France of the Fourth Republic, or by seemingly endless one-party government, as in the Fifth Republic of Gaullist France. Where Parliament seems to offer few satisfactions, trade unionism can be an alternative. The great national strikes in France in May 1968 expressed just this sort of disappointment with traditional democratic methods. And so, in a quite different way, did the decisions of the Dutch Socialist trade unions in 1972 to make an anti-inflation deal with the employers that included a number of important social reforms, while the politicians were attempting to put together yet another coalition government.

In spite of their propaganda, the unions are certainly far more pragmatic in their day to day activities than their formal differences would lead one to expect. Italian unions regularly negotiate together and the French CGT (communist) can and does publish common platforms with the CFDT (socialist) on everything from immigration to pensions. Doctrinal disagreement may mask practical agreement on specific issues, but it does not prevent it.

And there is another paradox which it would be unwise to overlook. A militant ideology can conceal a strongly pragmatic streak, and a moderate ideology can, equally, hide an extremely impractical union character. Thus in France and Italy, employers often prefer to deal with the allegedly revolutionary communist unions, because, they say, these unions drive a hard bargain but at least they stick to it when they have made a deal; whereas the non-communist unions lack the discipline to make any bargain effective. In countries like Britain and Ireland where the marxist tradition has not taken root, on the other hand, the presence of communists in a union negotiating team is seen by the employers' side—usually rightly—as a factor likely to make a bargain hard to reach and even harder to enforce once it is made.

At the beginning of this chapter I quoted a remark about the pluralism and diversity of the tiny Luxembourg union movement. At the end, it is worth quoting the sentence that followed:

'However, since the end of the war, united trade union action, even organic trade union unity, has become one of the permanent preoccupations of most trade union leaders.' They are, perhaps, beginning to realise that the only service to the worker the divisions between European unions render today is to make union membership lower than it would otherwise be. Workers increasingly fail to see why they should join a divided union movement and their leaders may now be starting to listen to them.

Notes

For the section on the development of the German trade union movement I am indebted to the *History of the German Labour Movement*, Helga Grebing, Oswald Wolff, London, 1969. Other principle sources include: *The Trade Union Movement in the European Communities*, EEC Press and Information Department, Brussels 1972; *Unions in Europe*, by Eli Marx and Walter Kendall, Centre for Contemporary European Studies, University of Sussex, Brighton, 1971.

1. 'History and Structure of the Luxembourg Trade Union Movement', *The Trade Union Movement in the European Communities*, *op. cit.*, p. 1.
2. *Fraternization*, 5 November 1841, cited by Grebing, *op. cit.*, p. 30.
3. Appeal to Union Members, 1891, cited by Grebing, *op. cit.*, p. 68.
4. Report on Activities (1969–71) to 10th World Congress of the International Confederation of Free Trade Unions, London, July, 1972, ICFTU, Brussels, p. 23.

3 *Structure and Penetration*

The history and the present structure of the trade union movements in Europe look extraordinarily confused and diverse. At first glance, it almost seems as if the movements of no two countries have anything in common—the one exception that struck me to begin with being the fact that everywhere print workers are among the first, if not actually the very first, groups of workpeople to form trade unions, and in every national league table of wages they come at or near the top of the list of well-paid blue-collar workers. (No doubt there is a connection between the two —early unionisation, itself the result of the early industrialisation of the industry, and, probably, a direct if shadowy descendant of the old guild system, had given printers a grip on their jobs which they had kept and used to secure the best wages.) But apart from this interesting but admittedly rather peripheral point, differences seemed far more evident than similarities.

Even the terminology is difficult. Does a dictionary translation carry the same significance from one language to another? I remember an especially puzzling first conversation with a French trade union official, who told me there were several thousand *syndicats* affiliated to the CFDT. Several thousand unions—wasn't that what *syndicat* meant? It took quite some time to work out that what he understood by *syndicat* was what I understood by the term union branch; what I called a union, he called a *fédération*; while the CFDT itself—like the FO and the CGT—was to him a *confédération*.

The confusion is understandable but it can be exaggerated and some of it at least can be cleared away. For one thing, many of the ideas behind trade unionism have been transplanted directly from one country to another and are common to all. No country has developed its union system to the present day in complete isolation. In the case of Sweden, for instance, the first attempts at unionisation were helped by the Danish labour movement, which had set up a special branch precisely to provide support for their neighbours. And later, the first of the major efforts between the two World Wars to reach fundamental agreement between the two sides of Swedish industry was inspired by the (as it turned out, abortive) example of the talks with the trade unions initiated in England by Sir Alfred Mond following the 1926 British General Strike. In addition much of the specific character of each country's unions depended on the date and the nature of its industrialisation, and the political and legal background against which it took place.

But, more important, though there were striking differences between countries they were differences that could be seen as revolving around common themes; and no matter what particular type of structure had evolved, each is today faced with similar problems and limitations. A fairly detailed description of the union organisations in two countries—Ireland and Sweden—will show just how diverse union structures can be, and at the same time give a first basis for discussing some of the problems that are common to most European movements.

Ireland

For a country with so small an employed labour force as Ireland—under three-quarters of a million—there is certainly an astonishingly large number of trade unions, 123 by one count. There is a bewildering variety of unions, both constitutionally and in terms of membership. The reason lies partly in the type of trade unionism inherited from days when Ireland was part of Great Britain and is partly the result of the complex links that still exist between the two countries, not the least of which is the ambiguous status of the North.

Thus, of the 123 unions with members in the Irish Republic some twenty-nine have their headquarters in Britain. Of the ninety-four with headquarters in the Republic itself, only three have members in the North, while all twenty-nine of the British-based unions have members in both parts of the country. (A few unions have their headquarters in the North, but none of these have members in the South.)

In order to negotiate in the Republic, unions need to be

licensed, but in order to be licensed they must be registered under Irish law. British unions are not so registered; instead, they get around the licensing problem by paying a deposit to the Irish High Court. Registration gives unions a number of advantages, such as tax exemption on their benefit funds and a good deal of immunity from legal intrusion into their internal affairs. The effect of all this is that unions operate under a number of legal forms. As one writer has put it, they may be 'unregistered and unlicensed, unregistered and licensed, registered but unlicensed and registered and licensed'.[1]

If the Irish unions are a legal mixture, they are an even greater organisational mixture. They do not easily fit into the traditional descriptive categories of craft, industrial and general unions. The three types are all represented, but the first two at least are distinctly blurred. Craft unions, set up to protect the exclusive interests of occupational groups, have been diluted by the admission of unskilled workers, while such industrial unions as exist, for example, in the footwear industry, are not true to the definition of industrial unionism—that one union alone should cater for all the workers in a given industry—since no industrial union actually sits down to negotiate with the employers on its own; it always shares power at the bargaining table with at least one other union.

Attempts to categorise Irish unions along traditional lines leave so many organisations in limbo that the Irish Congress of Trade Unions (ITUC) has itself attempted a seven-part breakdown: general unions; unions of manual workers (subdivided into craft and mixed); postal unions; civil service organisations; distributive and office workers; insurance and bank employees; professional and service workers. These are hardly very bold descriptive terms, but they seem to be the only way in which the Irish unions can accurately be categorised.

So far as the degree of trade union penetration goes, Irish unions have done well by European standards, with over 50 per cent of the employed population in union membership. This is particularly impressive when it is remembered that Ireland has proportionately the largest rural population in Europe and much of its new industry has been introduced into areas without an industrial and so trade unionist tradition. It also seems likely that white-collar employees, though making up only about a fifth of the total number of trade unionists, are as well organised as manual workers in proportion to their numbers in the employed population—again, a high proportion by European standards.

The Irish trade union movement stands squarely inside what might be called the Anglo-Saxon tradition so far as its internal distribution of power is concerned. There is only one major union centre (though there is also a small, twenty-member professional grouping) and it does not have strong political or ideological commitments on the Continental pattern. But neither does it exercise much central authority. Unions have complete bargaining freedom and are scarcely subject to any sanctions from the ITUC. The ITUC, like the British TUC, can threaten expulsion in an extreme case, but it depends very much on the goodwill and co-operation of its member unions to carry out its policies. The one area in which the individual unions have handed over power to the central body is in questions of inter-union dispute, which are clearly something of a probability given the irregular structure of the union movement. And in recent years, the ITUC has conducted central negotiations with the Irish employers' union over wage guidelines.

The basic unit in the Irish movement is the branch, usually based on a geographical area, though sometimes on an industrial plant or workshop. Occasionally branches may have almost the autonomy of an independent union, but in the main they are subject to the authority of the union executive, certainly in questions of industrial action. At factory level, workers are represented by elected shop stewards, but these do not yet seem to have developed the power of initiative that local union representatives have evolved elsewhere, though it is increasing. In many cases their function is little more than that of dues collectors. Actual negotiation is conducted by the national unions with the result generally subject to the balloted approval of their memberships, and in the overwhelming number of cases negotiations are at the level of the individual firm and not of the industry as a whole. Only some 20 per cent of workers are covered by industry-wide deals. Even in nationalised concerns, overall negotiations are limited to the rates for unskilled and semi-skilled men; craftsmen in these enterprises normally follow the rates negotiated for similar work locally in private industry.

The main characteristics of the Irish movement can now be summed up. It has grown piecemeal over the years, unions being created as the need for them arose. Rationalisation of union structure has been discussed from time to time but nothing much has come of it, apart from a number of mergers and the establishment of joint negotiating bodies linking two or more unions, as the bargaining situation has required. The emphasis of union aims has been on the extension of collective bargaining, usually fairly narrowly defined to cover little more than improvements in the terms and conditions of employment. Bargaining has developed more or less untrammelled by institutional interference: there is a Labour Court, but it is mainly confined to the role of conciliator or mediator; works councils do exist but they are scattered, infrequent, voluntary and not much regarded. Central authority is weak, the national union centre having only the ultimate sanction of expulsion and little except influence to yield, except over inter-union disputes. The unions themselves have limited authority over their own members, though full-time officials are generally appointed by the union executive and, where the closed shop exists, some discipline in relation to individual members may be implicit in the possibility of depriving the individual of his membership and therefore his job. The shop steward system has not yet become the direct challenge to union authority that it often seems in Britain. Foreign influence is unusually strong, not only because the Irish system was largely derived from that of its former ruler, Britain, but because a substantial number of unions are still 'foreign-based', that is, have their headquarters in London—a situation perhaps only paralleled by the importance of American international unions in Canada.

Sweden

In contrast to the Irish movement, the Swedish trade unions appear to have developed in distinct stages towards an orderly form of structure. Major events have led to major reassessments of aims and methods, resulting in a more powerful, a more rationally organised, certainly a richer, union movement.

Some of the stages in the Swedish development are worth recording, if only for the light they cast on the movement's approach and attitudes. In the early days, in the 1880s, the union federations had no common organisation of their own. The embryo Social Democratic Party served as their central board. When the Swedish Trade Union Confederation, the LO, was founded in 1898 there was a move to make affiliation with the party a condition of membership. Several unions declined and the proposition was dropped, though there remain strong links between the unions and the party.

The employers' central organisation, SAF, was founded in 1902, following a three-day strike by some 150,000 workers over parliamentary suffrage, and four years later, after an eight-month strike by some 30,000 metal workers, the LO and the SAF reached an agreement under which the employers accepted the unions as negotiators while the unions in return acknowledged the employers' basic right to hire and fire. Three years later a third major strike, which ended in a crushing defeat for the unions, taught both sides new lessons. The employers did not press their advantage to the point of extinguishing the unions completely, as perhaps they might have done; they seem to have foreseen the need for unions to continue to exist as bargaining agents in an increasingly industrialised society. And for their part, the unions were compelled to think seriously about their structure—which, as elsewhere, had originally been a mosaic of craft and local organisations—if only because some unions had been eliminated altogether by the strike. Because of this (and also to some extent under the influence of syndicalist ideas of the unions achieving ultimate worker control of industry by means of a decisive general strike) the LO opted for a system of industrial unionism that is still the pattern today.

In 1932, a predominantly social democratic government was elected for the first time (social democrats have been in power continuously ever since) and two years later the unions were again confronted with a problem arising from a major strike. This time it was because of a proposed cut in wages in the building industry.

The unions' natural instinct was to support their building worker colleagues, but when the strike dragged on another side of the situation grew in importance. The government was trying to stimulate economic activity through the provision of new construction work. It was a policy the unions strongly supported because of the jobs it would provide, but it was evidently not going to be effective while the industry was at a standstill. Eventually, the LO put pressure on the building workers to settle— at a not notably high price.

The political and industrial situation now gave both sides something to think about. The trade unions realised that there was more to solidarity than merely backing the wage claims of one group of workers and, while government intervention might have been good for them so long as it was done by a socialist government they could hardly know then how long the Social Democrats would survive. The same thought, but the other way about, struck the employers. The upshot was that both sides discovered they had something to gain by agreeing between themselves on voluntary methods of regulating their relations, rather than leaving regulation to the government of the day. This realisation prompted two years of negotiation, leading to the Basic Agreement of 1938 which, in revised form, is still the foundation of relations in industry.

These incidents illuminate the character of Swedish trade unionism, revealing it as voluntarist, aiming to keep the government as far as possible out of union affairs, but at the same time highly centralised and self-disciplined. The LO exercises much more influence than most national union centres. It conducts regular outline negotiations with the SAF along lines agreed with the unions, leaving individual unions to negotiate only within a set framework (for example, giving priority in one round of negotiations to a certain category of worker). It lays down standard statutes for member unions, to which they have now adapted their own statutes. It has the duty of financially backing strikes by affiliated unions, and thus by extension the right to veto strike proposals. (No union can authorise a strike by more than three per cent of its membership without the agreement of the

LO executive board, and the LO has the right to be represented during bargaining by a member union.) It has a strong influence over union structure, periodically drafting new proposals concerning organisation and retaining the power to allocate the rights to represent groups of workers as between unions. Finally, it has made a whole series of central agreements on non-wage matters with the SAF, on subjects like safety, training, time and motion studies and the employment of women—issues which in other countries are usually dealt with either at industry level or by central government.

What goes for the LO also goes for the individual unions which comprise it. Under the statutes that are common to all LO unions, each union must have an executive right of veto over strike action—groups of workers cannot go on strike without the approval of their executives—and union executives exercise a final right of decision over all negotiated agreements. Further, the unions have so far sunk their natural rivalries as to agree to a common wage policy—the so-called 'solidarity' policy—dating back to 1936, under which the joint aim is to close the gaps between the wages of different groups of workers, though not without consideration of the requirements of different types of work. (This policy survives, but, as we shall discover later, it has run into difficulties in recent years as a result of pressures from higher paid workers afraid of being robbed of their privileges by, on the one hand, the wages of the lower paid catching up with their own and, on the other, progressive taxation.)

At the local level, the basic unit of organisation is the branch, but in Sweden this is largely an administrative body concerned with such matters as dues collection and the payment of benefits; the branch does little negotiating. In the factory, negotiation— usually over the interpretation of national wage agreements—is conducted by the factory club. There are no shop stewards as there are in Britain—the chairman of the factory club is his nearest equivalent—though there are works councils in factories with more than fifty employees. The works councils are not, however, bargaining agencies, but deal with relatively uncontroversial matters like training and production. Being administrative and not bargaining units, branches are hardly subjects of political controversy. It has therefore been comparatively easy for the LO unions to cut the number of their branches by well over half since 1945, the aim being purely and simply to make branches big enough to support full-time staff, and thus release officials for more important work.

Union membership is high—in some industries reaching to as much as 98 per cent, and LO unions covering in all some 47 per cent of the population—in spite of the fact that there is no closed shop system (with the strange exception of the hairdressing trade, where an agreement among organised master-hairdressers is matched by one among their employees; the hairdressers will only work for, and the master-hairdressers will only employ, those who are organised). There is a trend, though, partly as a result of labour shortages, for employers to encourage union member-ship, since workers who are scarce but non-unionised can be difficult to deal with, while unions provide at least a channel for discussion.

The unions' pragmatic approach, their willingness to learn from experience, their sense of partnership in the economy and society—all this does not mean that they have solved every one of their problems. For instance, although the LO policy is one of strict industrial unionism, it has not been fully achieved. In metal and wood, industrial unionism is clear cut; but in transport, unions are divided, largely along the lines of who happens to own the various elements in the transport system. There are similar divisions within the government service, although not in local government. And it is not true, as it is often thought to be, that only one union covers all the employees in a Swedish plant or factory. Foremen and higher grade employees are generally organised in separate unions, which in turn belong to a different national union centre, the Central Organisation of Salaried Employees (TCO), and this can lead to inter-union rivalries and disputes. There are, in fact, no fewer than five union confederations in Sweden. Apart from LO and TCO, these are SACO, for professional workers, SR, for civil servants, and SAC, the rump of the early twentieth-century anarcho-syndicalist movement. For all its apparent haphazard and erratic growth, the Irish labour movement has at least avoided this kind of split.

As should now be clear, there are wide differences between the Swedish and the Irish union movements. The Swedish is wealthy, centralised, disciplined but divided along mainly occupational lines; the Irish has little central control, shows no signs of having been thought through or planned, but contrives to unite all but a very small fraction of the union interests in the country. (No doubt it is the very lack of central authority or ideology that has made it possible for almost every Irish union to shelter under the same umbrella.) But in spite of the differences, a comparison between them does reveal some of the problems of union organisation that are common to both, and to most of the movements in Europe. These are: the degree of penetration achieved by unions among the employed population in their countries, that is, the rate of union membership; the type of organisation; and the distribution of power within unions.

Membership

No matter what sort of union movement there may be, it seems difficult for any of them to win even half the employed population into membership. Comparative international statistics are notoriously hard to analyse, and not least those of trade unions in different countries since methods of counting heads vary from place to place and unions have a habit of exaggerating their numbers in order to make their strength seem the more impressive. In the selected table that follows, a particularly reserved view should be taken of the figure for Italian union membership, which is notoriously prone to inflation.

Country	Union membership density
Germany	37%
France	20%
Italy	57%
Netherlands	42%
Belgium	66%
Luxembourg	50%
United Kingdom	46%

(Source: European Community Statistical Office, cited by Coventry Engineering Employers' Association.)[2]

One of the reasons for low union membership, ideologically divided trade unions, was discussed in the last chapter. The industrial structure of a country may also help to explain the degree of recruitment. Some industries lend themselves more easily to organisation than others. The engineering and metal-working industries, for example, appear to be highly organised throughout Europe. The fast-growing service sector, on the other hand, is a much less fertile source of members. It almost looks as if there may be a natural limit to union recruitment at around or below half the working population.

The one country that has significantly broken through the 50 per cent barrier is Belgium, even though it suffers from a union movement divided on religious and political lines. In Belgium, though, there are specific advantages in union membership that do not occur elsewhere. Some social benefits are paid exclusively to union members and not at all to the unorganised. The unions are authorised to act as agents for some social benefits; health payments, for instance, can be distributed through union assurance societies and unions may pay out unemployment benefits as well. Thus, whereas in most countries a period of high unemployment is usually marked by a drop in union membership, the reverse can and does happen in Belgium.

Type of organisation

The examples of Ireland and Sweden suggest something of the range of union structures in Europe. But, to risk a generalisation, the characteristic form of organisation in Europe as a whole is predominantly on an industrial basis. In France, for example, each of the three main union confederations—communist, ex-Christian and social democratic—has roughly the same number of member industrial federations (unions), approximately forty in each case. In Italy, the position is much the same. In Germany, the unions decided on an industrial structure immediately after the Second World War and there are only sixteen unions within the DGB, with the distinct possibility of mergers leading to even fewer unions in the near future.

Industrial unionism, in fact, seems to be closely associated with the centralised type of union movement. In countries like Britain or Ireland, where the national centre is little more than a co-ordinating body wholly dependent on the willing consent of its member unions and unable to exercise more than a narrowly limited authority over them on mainly inter-union questions, it is obviously impossible to impose a uniform structure on the original mass of local and craft unions spawned by gradual industrialisation. A certain amount of rationalisation has taken place, though with a minimum of direction from the centre. But where there is a strong central authority—created by political initiative, as in France and Italy, or born out of crisis, as in the Netherlands and Germany at the end of the War and, less dramatically, in Sweden—a planned pattern is obviously much easier to impose. (As always in trade union affairs, there are exceptions to any generalisation. Denmark, for one, has a powerful central body in its LO, at any rate where wage negotiation is concerned, but it has retained a good deal of the older type of union structure, mustering fifty unions in its LO to represent fewer than a million members.)

But the merits of one system against another remain controversial and a subject of endless debate (as it has been intensively debated for a decade or more in the British movement without any conclusive answer being reached). There is no ideal model, and the needs of any existing system are likely to change as old industries and skills decline and new ones rise. What is now a far more lively issue is the viability of present structures of whatever kind they may be. Are they sufficiently responsive to their members? Do they correspond with the new realities, especially those of emerging shop-floor power?

The distribution of power

The Netherlands has for much of the postwar period successfully worked an extremely centralised system of wage bargaining, first through a government-appointed board of conciliators who had to agree a change in wages, and later through a tri-partite social and economic council. This was made possible by the authority exercised over union members by the union leadership. A number of reasons have been cited for this.[3] The confessional unions were originally quite deliberately subordinate to the Church hierarchies. The socialist union (NVV) emerged in its centralised form from its early battles with the anarchically disposed syndicalists. The unions have large funds at their disposal and are involved in all kinds of social and cultural activities; union bureaucracies offer a career, with good financial prospects. Congresses of union delegates are only held at three-yearly intervals and the major decisions in between are taken by the professional executive. All this naturally eased the problem of control over a national wages policy.

Nevertheless, the system broke down in the latter part of the 1950s, in part because of the competition in wages being offered to Dutch workers in neighbouring countries. Breakdowns have also taken place in what had been thought to be comparatively stable systems in other countries—in Italy in 1969, in Germany in the same year, in Sweden two years later and, most explosively of all, in France in May 1968. The immediate causes, the weight of the impact and the later consequences vary considerably from country to country, but one common theme throughout has been the loss of contact between union leaders and the shop-floor, between the bureaucracies and the rank and file. In each case, the experience has shown that unions did not know what their members wanted, were unable to foresee the upset and were therefore unable to do anything to head it off. It has been a sharp reminder of the limitations of all kinds of centralised trade unionism.

These events highlighted one of the principal defects of the kind of trade unions that are built or led from the top downwards rather than the other way about. In much of Europe, shop-floor organisation is crude and ineffective, incapable of reflecting the moods and feelings of the workers and conveying them to their leaders. The breakdowns that took place seem to have caught union leaders as unprepared as governments and employers.

Since they happened, unions have devoted much of their attention to repairing the gaps in their structure and in their communications.

While in Britain, factory representation is highly articulated through the shop steward system, in the rest of Europe this is rarely the case. Instead, relations at this level have often been largely left to works councils, even though these may be barred by law from negotiating on questions of substance. Works councils may have seemed likely to be effective when they were introduced—in most cases, soon after the Second World War—when co-operation within industry in the task of reconstruction was the prevalent mood. But they have stood the test of peacetime 'normality' badly, while at the same time their existence appears to have discouraged the unions from trying to build their own alternative shop-floor organisations.

In Germany, for instance, the law specifically enjoins the works council to promote peaceful co-operation within the enterprise; it provides that all workers, not just trade unionists, may vote in works council elections; and until recently it prevented union officials from entering a plant without the employer's permission. Under union pressure, some of these inhibitions on union activity have been eased, as they have in Italy and France. But it is proving a difficult business to build organisations inside the factory after so many years of neglect. In Italy, the internal committees have seized their opportunity to negotiate over the heads of the unions, and the unions are finding it difficult to recapture the initiative. In the Netherlands, union clubs have been set up with the apparent aim of establishing a new means of contact and negotiation between workers and management, by-passing the existing works council system, and this may fragment workers' efforts as well as provoking employer resistance. In France, the unions' attempts to establish their presence in the plant following the 1968 changes in the law that gave them the opportunity to do so seem to have resulted only in more confusion. There are now no less than three systems of representation in the factory—the works council, the elected *délégué*, and the union appointed representative.

We shall return to this subject later. In the meantime it is enough to note that the diversity of union structures in Europe has not prevented union movements from having at least one thing in common: the inability to channel satisfactorily a multitude of new shop-floor grievances. Centralised bureaucracies without adequate back-up among their rank and file have shown particular weaknesses, though there are signs that the lesson has been learnt and much energy is being spent on repairing old deficiencies, as yet with limited success. It may be that the apparently more haphazard and untidy structures of Britain—and Ireland—being based to a large extent on rank and file organisation and built from the ground upwards, will turn out to be more resilient, more capable of meeting change, than its more rational-seeming counterparts on the Continent.

Union Enterprise

Any account of union structure that left out all mention of the union-owned enterprises would be seriously incomplete. The German unions are by far the most spectacular entrepreneurs. The scale of their enterprises is matched only by the Swedish and the Israeli unions, but they are being studied in other countries, especially in Australia, and a brief description of them may illuminate the sort of area of activity that unions may turn towards in the future and indicate an important source of the unusual strength and power of the German labour movement.

Co-operative trading organisations are common in the Western world—in Germany, the first one was established the year after the pioneering enterprise was begun in Rochdale in England—and they are usually a part of, or at any rate associated with, the local labour movement. But they are owned by their members and not by trade unions, though trade unions encourage and support them. And in most countries in Europe the co-operative mission may be thought to have been to a great extent fulfilled; with the modernisation of private-enterprise retailing, their function of providing a cheap, profit-sharing alternative seems far less valuable. At any rate, most of them have been undergoing a crisis as private chain stores offer a better and a cheaper service, particularly in food. It has been the turn of the co-operative movement to re-examine its functions and to modernise itself in the face of new competition.

'Commonweal enterprises', as the German unions call their own businesses, are similar to the co-operatives, but significantly different. They are similar in that they enter a market previously dominated by private enterprise and try to influence it to the benefit of the working-class consumer. They are different in that they are wholly owned by the unions rather than by their own member-customers though the German co-operative movement also has some shareholdings. Although they offer services similar to private-enterprise firms and compete directly with them, they differ in their operations in one crucial respect—the willingness of their union-owners to accept a lower rate of return on their investment than would be acceptable to capital raised on the ordinary commercial markets. (Not that this notably impoverishes the unions. Quite apart from the funds they retain themselves, the union bank is capable of sustaining even a major strike for as long as three months.)

At the start, in the early twentieth century and even before this, the unions' aim was to provide additional services for their members, like the unemployment and other insurance benefits that unions typically provided everywhere, but they have grown formidably from that point. They now include the fourth biggest bank in Germany, the biggest insurance company (in terms of the life policies issued) the biggest property development company in Europe and one of the three largest travel companies in Germany. The union businesses are all in personal services of one kind or another; they do not go in for manufacturing. What tempts the unions into a field of activity is the failure of private sources to give their members an adequate service. The case of insurance may be taken as representative.

As the DGB now tells it, insurance entrepreneurs 'let nothing stand in the way of making a profit. Insurance companies paid exorbitant commission fees to their representatives, in order to induce them to conclude as many new contracts as possible. This led to promises made by these representatives that could never be kept. The companies asked for exaggerated premiums from

their policy holders. Any claim against the companies was for-
feited without compensation once the insured could not pay the
premium, even if this happened only once. Such practices led to
very high dividends for the shareholders of these companies.
However, poor policy holders suffered losses amounting to
millions of marks.'[4]

The unions got together with the co-ops in 1912 and started
the first of the *Volksfursorge* (People's Care) group of insurance
companies. Among its achievements the group claims to have
completely reformed the life insurance market; to have set up a
unique system of life insurance for those at risk during the First
World War; to have offered makeshift insurance to unemployed
policy holders during the inter-war depression; to have offered
the best plans for reconversion following the currency reforms of
1923 and 1948; and more recently to have offered very high profit
shares to policy holders—as much as 99.8 per cent. Its social commitment has extended to its own investment policy; 80 per cent
of its capital has been put into housing projects. The secret of its
success, besides the shareholders' readiness to accept a low return,
has been to mobilise trade unionists as its agents. Some 33,000
part-time time workers now sell its policies, and costs are considerably lower than those of a normal insurance company.

Banking and building have also been part of the German labour
movement long enough to rank as traditional activities. The
pre-war Dewog group, itself an amalgamation of older union
enterprises, had built 80,000 flats for workers before it was seized
by the Nazis, and in its postwar name of Neue Heimat, it has built
more than 380,000 apartments, including some 90,000 owner-
occupied houses. It now undertakes large-scale town-planning
work and has a growing overseas business.

The Bank für Gemeinwirtschaft (BfG), the union bank, is the
result of a 1958 merger between regional union banks. As well
as looking after the funds of its owner-clients, the other commonweal enterprises and the unions, the BfG conducts normal competitive banking business, though it also claims to offer special
advantages to its individual customers, especially union members.
It was, for example, the first financial institution in Germany to

offer the house-buyer a full mortgage in a single transaction—previously, mortgage finance had to be pieced together from a number of different sources. The Bank has also acquired something of a reputation as a company doctor. After saving the Stinnes group from near bankruptcy in the early 1960s by buying it, refinancing and reorganising it and then selling it off within a year, it was approached by many other businesses in trouble. The Bank refuses to intervene in the majority of cases—regretfully, because there are usually union members' jobs at stake.

As the pace-setter in a limited number of service markets, the commonweal enterprises have clearly done a useful job for trade unionists; as the repository of all the shareholdings of the DGB unions, it has helped to make the movement probably the richest in Western Europe (high union dues and the relative lack of need to finance strikes has helped, too). But these enterprises are not without their difficulties. Ironically, the employees of the Bank do not regard Heinz Vetter as a suitable person to be the Bank president, even though, wearing another hat, he is also president of the DGB and thus the bank workers' own supreme union leader. It seems that they do not consider him impartial enough for the job.

Notes

For the sections on Ireland and Sweden see: *Industrial Relations in Ireland: the background*, by David O'Mahony, Economic Research Institute, Dublin, 1964; and *Trade Unions in Sweden*, Bo Carlson, Stockholm, 1969.

1. O'Mahony, *op. cit.*, p. 8.
2. *Labour Relations and Employment Conditions in the European Economic Community*, Coventry and District Engineering Employers' Association, May 1972, p. 30.
3. Marx and Kendall, *op. cit.*, pp. 29–30.
4. *Gemeinwirtschaft*, Bank für Gemeinwirtschaft, Frankfurt, 1971, p. 9.

4 *The New Workers Power*

In Britain and America, the classic method by which unions recruit members is now well established. They pick out a plant—an office or a workshop—that looks ripe for trade unionism; they move in, make contact, recruit as many members as they can, perhaps set up a new branch. Then, when they think they have enough strength, they get in touch with the management. They demand first recognition, and when they have secured that, negotiation. It may be tough going to get one or both, but these are the essential first steps. After this, relations may be amicable enough, but before, unions can achieve nothing. There are, of course, many variations in practice. It is not unknown for employers to invite a union into their factory, especially if they foresee trouble, perhaps in the form of a more militant rival union. In the course of time, relations may develop on both sides to the point where the principal negotiations are carried out, not between union and firm, but between union and employers' association, across a whole industry. The law may facilitate the process, as recent legislation in Britain has tried to do, although the unions have refused to make use of it because they think the law's disadvantages exceed its attractions. But the basic practice of trade unionism is founded on face to face relations with management, whether it be round the bargaining table in negotiations affecting the pay rates of millions of men or in an argument between a shop steward and a foreman over, say, one worker's failure to clock in exactly on time.

To someone used to this tradition, anything else seems strange, almost unnatural. I recall when it was first brought home to me that other methods were possible. It was in conversation with the chief of one of the German labour courts. In Britain at the time, a change in the law that would compel employers to recognise trade unions under certain conditions was being actively discussed.

Did he have many cases of this kind to deal with, I asked the court official? None at all, he replied, because in Germany the problem simply did not arise. Unions were not recognised by firms, but by employers' associations. The union had scarcely any direct function to play at that level. Indeed, union officials were only then admitted to the plant with the employer's approval. The functions of the shop steward in the British system were discharged in Germany by the works council. The whole tradition was quite different.

It would be wrong to make too much of such differences as these between industrial relations systems. They certainly do not prevent the same sort of problems cropping up at the same time in all of them, nor the same union interests developing. But it would also be wrong to ignore the differences or play them down. Trade unions do not operate in a vacuum. They grow up against a background of national characteristics—legal, political, industrial, social—which help to shape their own special characteristics. The attitude of British law towards trade unionism can be described, crudely, as having been one of distaste at what, in the unions' formative years, seemed to the legal and political classes to be little better than a criminal conspiracy. The conspiracy had to be permitted, if only because it was too powerful to abolish, but the unions were given few positive rights and few obligations towards society were imposed on them, and the attitude of the law has not changed much. This does a lot to explain what to most people outside Britain seems the chaotic and anarchic style of British trade unionism. When governments in the late 1960s and the early 1970s tried to reform the British unions by legal means, it was too late. The unions had thought of themselves as 'outlaws' for too long to be ready to let themselves be governed by the law.

In other countries in Europe, on the other hand, the legislators had tried to play a more active role. In many places, governments introduced works councils by law. Because of this unions had been discouraged from building their own organisations on the shop-floor. There was no need for unions to have relations with individual managements; that could be left to the works councils.

Hence the reply of the German labour court chief to my question about whether he had to deal with union recognition cases.

There are many other material differences in the contexts within which unions work, some imposed on them from outside, others proposed by the unions themselves and adopted, more or less to the unions' satisfaction, by governments and employers. Voluntary or not, they set the framework for trade union activity and do much to account for the variations in union styles and methods between one country and another. In this chapter I propose to discuss briefly the impact of the variety of forms that have been given to one basic legal right—the right to strike—and at greater length the means by which different union movements and governments try to interpret and promote the current general demand in Europe for increased worker power.

The Right to Strike

Union power, like any other, is ultimately based on the ability to deploy sanctions, in their case the strike. The freedom to strike is articulated in some legal form throughout the European democracies, but the precise form varies significantly and with important consequences.

In France and Italy, 'the freedom to strike belongs to a political tradition; it is seen as a human right, comparable to the freedom of speech or the freedom of association' and it is 'guaranteed by the constitution'.[1] Thus, in France the freedom to strike over-rides most other obligations even, for example, a procedural agreement inhibiting strike action until certain stages of negotiations or conciliation have been gone through, and other statutory conciliation procedures. And a French worker need not fear the sack for taking part in collective industrial action. If he individually operates an overtime ban, then he might be in breach of contract; if he joins in a strike, however, he is merely exercising his constitutional rights. As in Italy, a strike is 'not a breach of contract, but merely its suspension'.[2] And in Italy, the lockout is not an equivalent right; its use can be a breach of contract.

In Germany, by contrast, there is no constitutional right to strike action comparable to that in Italy or France, though there are rights of association in unions. The distinction drawn is therefore in effect the difference between the political right to strike and the right to strike only over economic questions. In West Germany, 'through the creative [or, as others would see it, destructive] activities of the Federal Labour Court [strongly influenced by academic opinion] a purely economic concept of the freedom to strike was introduced, so much so that no strike is now considered as "socially adequate" and therefore lawful, unless it is aimed at an act of collective bargaining'.[3]

Furthermore, 'the peace obligation is implied in all collective agreements. It need not be expressed. For the duration of the agreement the parties undertake not to resort to hostile action concerning any questions regulated by the agreement'.[4] It would seem, indeed, that even if an agreement specifically excluded any obligation to keep the peace, it would not stand up in the German courts.

There is also a peace obligation in Swedish labour law which prohibits industrial action during the life of a collective agreement. The Swedish law enumerates the circumstances in which strikes are unlawful:

1. On account of a dispute respecting the validity, existence or correct interpretation of the agreement, or on account of a dispute as to whether a particular action constitutes an infringement of the agreement or the provisions of the act; 2. In order to bring about an alteration of the agreement; 3. In order to enforce a provision which is to come into operation on the expiration of the agreement; or 4. In order to assist others in cases in which those others may not themselves commit offensive actions.[5]

Unlike France and Italy, in Britain and America the freedom to strike has evolved as 'a series of exemptions from civil or criminal liabilities';[6] there is no right to strike as such.

Too much stress should not, perhaps, be put on these differences. In every country, even where there is a constitutional right to strike, some legal limitations have been placed on the exercise of strike action. In France and Italy, strike freedom is not now extended by the courts to political strikes, and in Britain, the Industrial Relations Act of 1971 sought to make illegal certain strikes connected with, for example, recognition of closed shops, or against secondary targets, such as a supplier or customer of an employer with whom a union had its real dispute. Whether these restrictions are or can be effective is another matter. In modern circumstances it is hard to distinguish between a political and a merely economic strike. If the government is trying to run a policy of wage limitation, is it a political act to strike for higher wages? In Britain, the new strike laws themselves have in their first year probably caused more days to be lost through strikes than they saved by their prohibitions; few employers were willing to risk taking a union to court to find out if the law would be effective, and those who did—especially in the docks industry—found they had provoked more ill-feeling than they had resolved. Strikes can break out anywhere without too much regard for the legal niceties.

All the same, the legal framework that surrounds an industrial relations system must help to mould it into shape. There is no doubt that the political right to strike action, which is itself associated with a politically oriented trade union movement, is matched by a liberal use of that right by the Italian and French trade unions, while equally it is true that the peace obligations imposed upon German and Swedish labour by law correspond to the fact that industrial relations in both countries are among the most peaceful, the least strike-prone, in Europe. If no strict cause-and-effect relationship can be shown between the law and the industrial record, nevertheless it is reasonable to suppose that the law has had its effect.

Everywhere, workers and their unions aim to expand their influence and limit the power of the employer over their lives. Seen in this light, for example, claims for higher wages which most people, including many trade unionists themselves, regard as the main task of unions, are only one way towards achieving this more general aim—the more money a worker has, the greater independence he can achieve from his employer and the fuller his life is likely to be away from his work. In industrial society, increased income is a form of emancipation.

But, though rates of pay remain central, workers and unions are interested in more than that. In the factory, they want to have rights to a say in such matters as the pace of work, changes in production methods, hiring and firing, promotion policy, safety and health and dozens of other major and minor matters. Beyond conditions in the workplace, they also demand a voice in decisions affecting important elements of industrial or company policy, long-term planning, investment and, especially, decisions to close old and to open new plant. On top of this, of course, unions have ambitions that cannot be determined within industry alone; they need political action at the local as well as the highest government level. This is why the unions in all countries are closely associated with politics in one way or another. But politics are outside the scope of this discussion, though even here it is worth noting that some of the institutions that have been created to serve workers' ends and which will be described in this chapter were only secured after intensive political action: for example, in Germany at the beginning of the 1950s the unions only had their co-determination demands accepted by the government by threatening large-scale strikes and in Sweden in the 1930s the Basic Agreement was only reached under the threat of government legislation as an alternative.

The aim of extending workers' rights is common ground to all union movements, even if the precise list of demands and the scale of priorities varies from place to place. But the methods of achieving the common aims are strikingly unalike. In Britain and America the unions have had no affection for any institution that stands between them and the employer, in other words that gets in the way of straightforward, face to face collective bargaining. To the union movements in both countries, the best way to advance the workers' cause is to expand the area of collective bargaining. In most of Europe, on the other hand, there are numerous institutions that intervene in areas of union interest. Those that will be discussed here are the works council and the

organs of what—in Germany, where it is most fully developed—
is known as 'co-determination', of which the most significant
aspect is the presence of worker representatives on the supervisory
boards of companies.

Works Councils

The concept of workers' councils dates back a long way. In
Germany, they were first proposed as long ago as 1848 when they
were demanded by the Constitutional Assembly meeting in
Frankfurt during the revolutionary struggle that then affected
much of Europe. The First World War brought some new developments in co-operation between the two sides of industry,
but it was not until the Second World War and its aftermath that
joint committees were set up on a wide scale to discuss questions
other than pay and working conditions.

War brings special imperatives. The British engineering industry
in 1942 established a system of joint production committees by
agreement, from which wages and other subjects of collective
bargaining were deliberately excluded. The results have been
described in this way: '. . . the widespread adoption of the machinery through which, for the first time, the workers counted as
something more than mere factors of production, helped to secure
a rapid translation of their traditional hostility towards increased
production into widespread enthusiasm to assist the war effort.'[7]
Even in Britain, the mood which had produced this co-operation
survived the war but, though many joint committees continue
today, they are by and large ineffective. They remain in form
only; the substance of worker interest has been transferred to
collective bargaining.

Elsewhere, however, the promotion of new forms of joint
consultation apart from the old bargaining relationship were more
vigorously promoted. Agreements between the central union
and employer organisations to set up works councils were reached
in Sweden (1946), in Norway (1945) and in Denmark (1947); while
laws to establish them were passed in Germany (1952), in Belgium
(1948) and in the Netherlands (1950).

Whether established by law or not, the works councils were in most cases under similar rule. They were elected by all the workers in an enterprise; trade unions had little or no standing in them; they kept clear of wage questions; they did not negotiate or bargain or promote strikes. On the contrary, their object was to promote peace. According to the Netherlands law, the task of the works council was 'with due recognition of the autonomous function of the employer, to contribute its utmost to the best possible functioning of the enterprise'.[8] In Norway, the aim was 'through co-operation to work for the most efficient production possible and for the well-being of everybody working in the undertaking'.[9] And in Sweden to 'fulfil the function of working for greater productivity and greater occupational satisfaction. In so doing it is the duty of the council to maintain continuous collaboration between employer and employees'.[10]

These seem fairly anodyne objectives, something to which everyone could accede but few care deeply about, meaningful perhaps, in the early years after the war when the spirit of co-operation in economic reconstruction was still alive, but hard to recapture twenty-five years later. At any rate, by the end of the 1960s they were being judged a failure. An OECD report of 1969 said:

No matter how works councils have been conceived—as complementary to collective bargaining, or as a permanent problem-solving institution—in Western European industry they have been a failure. The socialist objective of making them an agent of control over management has not been achieved. The Catholic and Protestant objectives of satisfying the workers' basic needs of self-determination and freedom has not been achieved either. In most countries, workers' reactions to the councils are overwhelmingly negative.

Why was this? According to the report, one important reason 'if not the most important reason for the councils' failure, and for the failure of any consultative system, is the *complete lack of decision-making power* ... The consultative machinery is basically a talkshop, with little or no effect upon top decision-making, as well as upon the workers' participation in the organisation of their work, or in the preparation for the introduction of change'.[11]

This judgement on works councils seems to have been fairly widely accepted, but it does not mean that the experiment is over. The last few years have seen a number of responses to the works councils' lack of success. Machinery has been radically revised, in some cases leading to a relative downgrading of the councils' importance, in others to the opposite. But in each case the move has been in the direction of increased worker—and union—influence. These are some of the ways in which change is being made.

Italy

The evolution of works council systems in Italy since the war has been erratic but the trend of development seems now to be clearly towards direct collective bargaining between unions and management, no matter what the formal pattern of factory-level councils may be.

The first step in creating an institutional framework came in 1943, after the collapse of the Mussolini regime, by a national agreement to set up 'internal commissions' (*commissioni interna*), subsequently revised three times and reaching its present form in 1966. At the end of the War, indeed, it appeared that worker involvement in company affairs might quickly be taken much farther. Management councils (*consigli di gestione*) were established to provide joint consultation on all management questions in the larger industrial enterprises, particularly in Northern Italy. And the Italian Constitution of 1948 laid down that 'for the purposes of the economic and social betterment of labour and in accordance with the needs of production, the Republic recognises the right of workers to participate, in the forms and within the limits specified by the law, in managing the enterprise'. (Article 46). However, with the change in the political climate after 1947, the management councils rapidly dwindled, and the principle of participation set out in the Constitution has never been translated into practice.

The internal commissions are made up and operate in the following way: in small firms with between five and forty employees a single delegate is elected, the size of the commission increasing with the size of the firm to a maximum of twenty-one members in firms with more than 40,000 employees; the commission holds office for two years and its members have special protection for one year after that—they cannot, for instance, be sacked or transferred without the agreement of their union. Lists of candidates for the commission are put forward by each of the three main union centres (CISL, CGIL, UIL). Elections are by all the firm's employees, on a basis of preferential proportional representation. Commission members are subject to normal working hours, have to ask management permission before they leave their work to undertake commission duties, have a notice board at their disposal and may call meetings of workers, though usually outside working hours.

Among the subjects with which the commissions deal are agreements on working hours and redundancy; social legislation, including health and safety; the application of trade union agreements and the settling of disputes that arise over their interpretation; and the organisation, supervision and improvement of welfare services.

From the start, though the commissions' function was nominally supposed to be no more than 'to assist in maintaining normal labour-management relations in the enterprise, in a spirit of co-operation and mutual understanding, thus ensuring the regular flow of production', they went in for bargaining and settlement of disputes. But in recent years their powers have been substantially altered. Under the 1966 agreement collective bargaining was transferred to the unions; the Workers' Statute (Act of 20th May, 1970, No. 300) gave unions for the first time the right to have their own representation in the enterprise through elected shop stewards and since then a new system of works councils (*consigli de fabbrica*) has begun to emerge.

A new distribution of power has thus started to take shape. Some of the tasks previously performed by the commissions are now done by the shop stewards. Management must now get the agreement of the stewards on the principle and the methods of making supervisory checks on personnel and on the installation of television monitoring equipment. Stewards now superintend safety and health measures, including accident prevention and occupational diseases. In a number of new agreements, shop stewards have taken over the job of administering the interpretation of national agreements in the plant. Where there are no stewards, the internal commissions may still carry out their old duties. Alternatively, on questions such as piecework or the introduction of new equipment or new methods of work, committees that may be manned on the workers' side by shop stewards can try to negotiate solutions where the internal commissions have failed.

The result of this has been a good deal of overlap and confusion between the tasks of the shop stewards and those of the commissions. So the new works councils have taken the stage, aiming to combine the legally-based activities of the shop stewards with the work of the commissions, which were set up by agreement. Various advantages are seen in these new bodies by the unions. Members of the councils are elected to speak for different groups of workers, and not from a common list of employees of the whole enterprise; the three union centres do not put up their own lists of candidates as they do for the commissions, but a single list agreed by all three (one of the fruits of the campaign for unification of the union movement as a whole); and in general, the unions see the councils as avoiding the dichotomy that arose when there were two channels of communication and negotiation between managements and workers—the commissions and the unions—by bringing the two forms of representation together into one.

The unions, understandably, welcome the new pattern because it enhances their standing in that increasingly important area of worker interest, events inside the enterprise. Management, conversely, regrets what is happening because, as the commissions turn into works councils with a strong union presence, they cease to be instruments of co-operation and peace and become potential sources of disagreement and conflict.

The broad trend, however, seems clear. Following the 'hot autumn' of 1969, the Italian unions are trying to combine to reflect more effectively the simmering shop-floor discontents that

that experience revealed. Parliament has helped by extending new rights to trade unions inside the factory and the unions have followed up this advantage by securing agreements with employers for new kinds of institution to represent workers at shop floor level in which they will play a much larger part. The aim is to make more and more questions, more and more employer prerogatives, the subject of negotiation; in other words, to expand the area of collective bargaining on something like the British and American model. Works councils in Italy are being created as a means of exercising union power rather than as a supplement to it, or as useful and valid institutions in their own right.

Norway

Two early attempts to establish works councils in Norway were largely unsuccessful, but in the 1960s the results were reviewed and a new start made. In 1973, a completely fresh style of factory council system was initiated which promises a broad extension of workers' rights in management affairs.

The first attempt was made in 1920 when a Works Council Act required the establishment of committees to co-operate on productivity problems. More than a hundred were set up but they came to very little. Managements did not like them and the trade unions were highly suspicious. A new move came in 1945 when the confederations of employers (NAF) and unions (LO) agreed to set up production committees. More than 1,000 of them were formed, but by the 1960s surveys showed the results to be patchy at best—about a third of all the committees were simply not operative. In 1966, the 1945 agreement was wound up and a new Co-operative Agreement was made.

Under this deal, works councils have to be set up in all businesses employing more than a hundred people (similar arrangements have been made to cover central and local government workers). Where there are up to 400 employees, management and labour have five representatives each on the council and where there are more than 400, each side has seven. In the smaller councils the chairman of the union club or branch is automatically a member of the workers' side, and in the larger firms the deputy chairman is a member as well. This is an innovation—previous councils and production committees were kept quite separate from the unions —and it is specifically designed to ensure that links are preserved between the unions and the councils to avoid any conflict of interests.

But it does not mean that the councils are empowered to handle the traditional collective bargaining questions such as wages and hours. These are left to the unions and to a quite separate procedure. The councils' business is advice and information. Among the subjects that come before them are: changes in production, rationalisation, the improvement of safety and health, and training. They may discuss wages and hours, but they may not make agreements on them, and the same is true of discipline and complaints by employees. Councils are entitled to the same information as shareholders get at their annual general meeting, and indeed they may be given more confidential information which they must keep as secret as management requires.

The councils meet during working hours once a month or every two months. Much of their work is delegated to sub-councils at department level, the aim being to ensure as much employee participation as possible. Minutes are taken, and in some cases printed and circulated to all employees.

In contrast to Italy, the Norwegian unions do not see the works councils as a threatening, rival source of power—they would hardly have agreed with the employers to their establishment if they did. The LO in fact sits with the employers on a central Co-operation Council, which promotes the successful operation of the works councils, and both sides of industry contribute extensively to training and research. The existence of the works councils is a testimony to the self-confidence of both sides and to their mutual good relations.

The Netherlands

Works councils were first established in the Netherlands informally after 1945, and then by law in 1950. The founding impulse was the same as elsewhere in Europe, the sense of social cohesion induced by the war and later economic reconstruction, but as elsewhere in Europe the practical experience of operating the councils did not come up to expectations. For one thing, although legally established, companies suffered no penalties if they failed to set up a works council; consequently many did not do so, particularly the small firms. For another, the councils were given only limited rights of consultation and advice on matters that were not the subject of collective agreements, such as holiday dates, shift arrangements, staff grievances and so forth. Surveys showed a familiar set of shortcomings. Staff members of the councils were not properly trained; management and workers took different views of the councils' functions, with the former regarding them as merely consultative and the latter as bodies designed to defend their interests.

As a result, the 1960s saw a long process of review culminating in a set of proposals for reform from the Social and Economic Council (an advisory body made up of trade unionists, employers and independent experts), which led to a whole series of new Acts that radically revised the approach not only to works councils but to company and industrial law as well. The net effect has been substantially to strengthen worker influence over management's power of decision.

The 1971 Works Council Act has made the establishment of councils compulsory. If an employer does not comply, the employees may take action against him in the courts. But the regulations regarding size have been changed. The 1950 Act specified works councils in firms with more than twenty-five employees. It was in the smaller firms, however, that the councils worked least satisfactorily. The new lower limit is set at a hundred employees while the Social and Economic Council considers what can be done about the firms that fall below this limit.

Works councils are now elected by all employees of voting age who have worked for the company for one year, though council members must have three years' service. The chairman of the enterprise is automatically chairman of the council. Council members may be absent from work on full pay for an agreed number of days each year, and it is proposed that they should all spend five days on a special training course during their two-year term of office.

The trade unions are involved in activities at enterprise level in two ways. First, it is generally the unions that present lists of candidates for council elections; thus a close tie is kept between union and council. And second, NVV, the largest of the three Dutch trade union centres, has since the beginning of the 1960s been forming 'enterprise groups'. Union members elect a contact committee and a contact officer. By March 1971, 207 such groups had been formed. The Dutch employers are unhappy at this development, foreseeing the groups as a possible challenge to the works council system, and arguing that this would be wrong since fewer than a half of Dutch workers are union members. But if the unions are making a bid to challenge the councils, the trend is not yet clear. At present, indeed, part of the groups' task is seen officially by the unions as encouraging the work of the councils.

The composition and methods of the councils have been changed to some extent, but the real change has been in the councils' powers. Workers are now recognised as being present not merely to listen and discuss—to consult—but to defend employee interests as well. This is implicit, for instance, in the new right of the worker members of the councils to meet without the chairman being present. The other important rights the workers have been given are the right to give their opinion in advance of certain decisions being taken and the right of joint decision with management on a limited range of matters.

One example of the change in emphasis is the question of information. All works councils, under any national system, need information from the company if they are to be in any way effective. This need is recognised, though always with the reservation that management is likely to have some information that it would be commercially harmful to make even semi-public. The Dutch reforms maintain this principle, but with an important qualification. It is now no longer the employer alone who can decide whether particular facts should be divulged to the councils. The employees have the right to appeal against the employer's decision in the courts.

The subjects on which management must now listen to the

works council's advice—though not necessarily act on it—include these: sale or transfer of the business; shutdown, in part or in full; substantial contraction or expansion; relocation; and certain items of special interest to the employees when they are not covered by a collective bargain, such as wage agreements, training, recruitment and dismissal. Missing from the list is the problem of redundancy. On this issue, the employers are expected to consult with the unions first, on the grounds that it would be next to impossible to expect the works councils to be discreet on something that so closely affects themselves and the people they represent.

The subjects on which management must not only listen to the works council but get its agreement before making any innovations or changes include pensions, hours, holidays, safety and health.

These are strictly limited areas of joint decision. There have been other advances in worker rights over management decisions, but at this stage it is necessary to mention only two. The first is where unions believe there is evidence of serious mismanagement of a company. With the approval of the works councils, the unions may now ask the courts to appoint a committee of inquiry into the company's affairs, which the courts must do unless they believe the request is manifestly frivolous. Subsequently, depending on the report of the committee and the demands of the union, the court may order a series of changes in the company management, from the reversal of certain decisions to the liquidation of the entire enterprise. The importance of this is seen to be rather as a deterrent to management than as a weapon that will actually be often used.

The last reform to be dealt with here concerns mergers. Where a merger is proposed involving a firm with more than a hundred employees, the unions must be notified and consulted over the implications for employees. This is not established by law; it is an agreed procedure whose rules are administered by a committee of the Social and Economic Council. If the rules are not observed the committee may publish a statement as a form of sanction, and undertakings have been given by stock market organisations that, following any such censure, their dealer members will not take part in transactions associated with the merger.

Germany

Works councils were first introduced into Germany under the Weimar regime in 1920, but when they were fully re-established after the Nazi period by the Works Constitution Act of 1952 it was on a subtly different basis. The pre-war councils were seen as instruments of negotiation and possible conflict; the post-war councils were designed to achieve reconciliation and peace.

The works council system seems to have worked more smoothly in Germany than in other European countries. At any rate, it has provoked less union hostility. The unions support the councils though they have had criticisms to make, some of which were met by a revision of the law in 1972.

Councils have to be set up in all establishments employing five people. Everyone over eighteen may vote providing they have worked for the company for six months, though supervisory staff—this includes senior staff without executive functions—are excluded. Voting is by secret ballot on lists put forward by the employees themselves; council members serve for three years. The size of the council depends on the number of the firm's employees. In the larger firms, or in companies which own more than one enterprise, there must be a central council. Council members have time off on full pay for their council duties and in large enterprises council officials may be permanently relieved from their work. The employer has to pay the council's costs and provide it with the necessary premises and other facilities. The council is enjoined to secrecy on confidential matters. Every three months it makes a report to a general meeting of all employees, during working hours, and employer representatives have to be invited to attend if they wish.

Before 1972, the unions were more or less rigidly kept away from the councils. The unions' sphere was held to be negotiation on wages and hours and other questions with employers' associations outside the enterprise, while the works councils dealt with problems inside the plant. Union officials had to ask the employer's permission before passing through the factory gates. The separation between unions and councils can be over-emphasised, however. Surveys have shown that the great majority of council members, especially the chairman of the workers' side, were union members; and the unions provided extensive training to prepare their members for council work. But the unions were given greater access by the 1972 law. Union officials need now only inform employers when they intend to visit a firm; they may attend works council meetings if this is agreed by one-quarter of the council members; and they may be present at the plant-wide three-monthly meetings already mentioned. The unions have certain rights to take initiatives where works councils have not been established before, and when a council is being elected for the first time it may put forward a list of candidates, though not at subsequent elections.

Previously, the works council had limited rights to information and consultation, but these have now been expanded to the point where, on certain matters, the councils have rights of veto or joint decision. Unless there is an over-riding legal or collectively bargained regulation, the councils have powers of joint decision with management on questions like starting and stopping times and work breaks; the use of mechanical means for measuring workers' performance; piece and job rate fixing; the time, place and method of making payments; and the establishment and running of welfare organisations.

On personnel questions, the councils have a variety of powers which together considerably inhibit traditional management rights. As a minimum, the works council has to be kept informed of personnel policies and it may require that vacancies be advertised internally, giving employees the first chance to apply for new openings. In enterprises with more than 1,000 employees, the council can ask for the general rules of personnel policy to be spelled out, and in any firm where there are such general rules the council has to give its consent to them. Over hiring and transfers the council can object to the employer's action, in which case the employer has to go to the Labour Court for approval (in urgent cases, he can act first, but the question still has to go to the Court), and the council has to be heard on all dismissals, otherwise the dismissal is unlawful and without effect. An employer can go ahead with a dismissal against the advice of the council, but when that happens the employee can insist on being kept on until the Court has had an opportunity of deciding whether the dismissal was justified or not.

Finally, when a company is planning major changes affecting employment—for example, substantial rundown or closure, merger or transfer, a fundamental switch in enterprise aims and methods—the works council has rights to information and consultation, and beyond that it may ask the employer to produce a social plan designed to minimise the effect of the changes on the workers. Among other things, the social plan could contain an order by which the firm proposes to dismiss redundant employees, so that older men and those with families come after the younger ones and the bachelors; and in it redundancy payments are set out. If the council does not approve the company's social plan, an arbitration committee decides. The employer may not then vary an agreed solution, except at the risk of being taken to court and compelled to pay his former employees for up to a full year.

The pattern of evolution of the works council in Europe should now be reasonably clear from these examples. Although they have earlier antecedents, they came into being in something like their present form during or after the Second World War. But the spirit of solidarity between workers and management that marked the period of their origin was dissipated in the years that followed. The councils were not capable of dealing with the new social strains, for which they were not designed. Responses differed. In some countries, the tendency was to replace them with trade union organisation and their functions with those of collective bargaining. In Britain, the joint production committees quickly fell into disuse and shop steward committees moved in. In Italy, more recently, in-plant consultative machinery has been converted, making it more like an instrument of collective bargaining and giving the trade unions a far stronger role. In other countries

—Germany, the Netherlands, Norway—the works councils have been reconstructed in such a way as to recognise, implicitly or explicitly, that workers' interests need to be articulated and protected and do not coincide with those of management, as the original constitutions of the councils suggested they did. In these countries, too, the trade unions have been given, or have assumed for themselves, a larger role at shop floor level than before, though they do not by any means have control of the works councils.

But however they have been reformed and improved, works councils and shop steward committees still have a severely limited scope. No matter how powerful, management still proposes and the workers' representatives still do no more than oppose, or at any rate argue. At best, they may have some limited rights of veto over management actions that prejudice workers' standards or employment. But works councils and shop stewards' committees do not influence policy at the formative stage; they merely react to policy when it has been made. In some countries, however, workers' organisations have tried to take the process a stage further by involving themselves directly in management at board and policy-making level. The demand for this is spreading but so far only the German trade unions have developed the fullest theoretical and practical experience. It will therefore be appropriate to examine first what has happened in Germany and then to look at ways in which similar themes are being developed in other countries.

Co-determination

For the German trade unions, co-determination is both an idea and a practical programme. The idea is, quite simply, to extend to industry the democratic emancipation the workers have already won in politics, through their right to vote; or, as the unions themselves put it, to change the situation whereby workers are 'political subjects' but 'industrial objects'.[12] The programme as it has developed so far has involved the construction of machinery through which workers' industrial interests can be represented. Its main elements are first the works councils, and second, and more distinctively, the presence of workers' representatives on company boards.

Both the idea and the programme have lengthy histories, though both have been substantially modified over the years. As happened in other countries, the German unions won their first important sharing of power during the First World War when, as a result of a Bill which they helped to draft, workers' committees were established in munitions' factories and the unions were recognised as equal negotiating partners with the employers at factory level. The Weimar constitution stated that 'the manual and non-manual workers are authorised, as equal partners with the employers, to participate in the determination of their terms and conditions of employment, and in the overall development of the productive forces of the nation. The organisations on both sides, and the agreements reached by them, enjoy legal recognition'.[13] In the 1920s, the outlines of the present system were already evident. Works councils were established by law in 1920, and later one or two council members were appointed to companies' supervisory boards. Workers were given a large measure of influence amounting virtually to control in a number of industries, including coal and potash mining, and in some firms a director resembling the present labour director was appointed. All this was, of course, swept away during the Nazi period.

Since the Second World War, co-determination has enjoyed broad political support. The Christian Democrats accepted it as a 'thoroughly justified and natural demand'[14] in 1951 though, not surprisingly, their practical enthusiasm proved to be less complete than that of the Social Democrats, whose programme to 1959 stated that 'democracy demands the co-determination of the workers in the enterprise and throughout the whole economy. The worker must no longer remain merely a subject of the economy; he must become a citizen of the economy. Co-determination in the iron and steel industry and in coal mining, is a beginning of a re-organisation of the whole economy'.[15] (But the Free Democrats oppose co-determination which has made it impossible for the Brandt Government—an alliance between Social and Free Democrats—to advance the unions' demands as far as the Social Democrats alone would have wished.)

Co-determination in its present form emerged from a series of Acts passed in the early 1950s—though not without some fairly militant pressure from the unions—and modified by the Works Constitution Act of 1972. The works council aspect we have already dealt with; the system of workers' representation on company boards remains to be described.

The practical application of this system is shaped by the structure of power in the German joint stock, or private limited liability, company. Such companies have a three-tier system of decision-making. At the top are the shareholders who act through the annual general meeting. Then there is the supervisory board (*aufsichtsrat*), which appoints the management board (*verstand*) and decides overall policy. Finally, there is the management board itself which is responsible for the day to day operation of the enterprise. Members of the supervisory board are never at the same time members of the management board.

Under the Works Constitution Act of 1952, the employees of a joint stock company, or of a private limited liability company, with more than 500 workers elect by ballot one-third of the members of the supervisory board. Most of the employee representatives are themselves employees, though, where there are several employee board members, only two need be—the others may be brought in from outside. They have the same rights and duties as the board members elected by the shareholders—like them, for instance, they have to keep secret confidential information.

The Co-determination Act of 1951 takes workers' representation a step further than this, but only in the iron, steel and coal industries. In other industries workers have only one third of the seats on the supervisory board, and therefore a limited influence on policy and appointments. But in iron, steel and coal, they have parity of representation with the shareholders, and therefore a much greater degree of influence. These industries were singled out for special treatment, in part because of the political role their former owners had played in bringing Hitler to power, and it was thought that a strong trade union presence at policy-making level would help to prevent this happening again; but the unions had to exert heavy pressure before the Christian Democratic Government of Dr Adenauer would accept it.

The supervisory boards of steel and coal companies have eleven, fifteen or twenty-one members. In an eleven-member board, the shareholders elect four members directly, plus a fifth who does not directly represent shareholder interests. The workers' side also has five members, of whom one is neither an employee nor a trade unionist, two are employees—one blue, one white collar—proposed by the works council after consultation with the trade union concerned, and two are nominated by the union. These ten members between them elect an eleventh, independent, board member. The independent member, together with the fifth member elected by each side, who are not direct representatives of each side's interests, are the so-called additional or further members and have the duty of representing the public interest, while also looking after the interests of the company. The board now constituted elects a chairman, usually one of the shareholder members. The board of management, which the supervisory board appoints, must include, as well as the usual technical and commercial directors, a labour director who has equal rights and responsibilities with his co-directors and who is in charge of labour and personnel questions. A labour director cannot be appointed or removed without the approval of a majority of the employees' side of the supervisory board. In other words, on this appointment the workers have a right of veto.

To complete the institutional picture, employees have the right to the establishment of a joint production committee through which information about the firm's performance can be passed; the Personnel Representation Act of 1954 gave to the public service most of the rights accorded private sector employees in the 1952 Act; and the rights of equal employee representation on supervisory boards of companies in the steel and coal industries have been extended to cover appropriate holding companies (which were prohibited under Allied legislation when the 1951 Act was passed).

Under the full system, the German workers have a formidable array of channels through which to express their grievances and solve their problems. They have their unions which, in negotiations with the employers' associations, set the basic pattern of wages and conditions; they have works councils, increasingly associated with the unions, which deal with the whole range of problems that occur on the shop floor; and they have influence in the boardroom in the form of either parity co-determination in the steel and coal industries, or, in other industries, of one-third of the members of the supervisory board. The DGB believes passionately in this pluralist approach and it evangelises for its extension; in Germany, by giving parity of votes to workers' representatives on the supervisory boards of all large companies (that is, those with either 2,000 employees, a balance sheet total of DM75 million, or an annual turnover of DM150 million), and in the rest of Europe by lobbying the Brussels Commission to include worker members in future on the boards of the European companies, as indeed the Commission has proposed in a draft statute.

Meanwhile, the concept of workers on boards, never previously very popular with trade unions outside Germany, has been spreading and is beginning to crop up not only in trade union programmes but in law as well. Other countries have adopted the idea to suit their own national circumstances and the local shades of trade union opinion. These are some of the most recent developments.

On 1 January 1973, an Act passed by the Norwegian Storting came into effect, bringing a new sort of council to about 1,000 Norwegian companies. These are the 'democratic factory councils' (*Bedriftsforsamlinger*) which have to be established in all companies with above 200 employees. The councils must have at least twelve members, of whom one-third are themselves employees, elected by the employees. It is this factory council which elects the company board; the employees have the right to elect one-third of the board members with a minimum representation of two. The other important function of the new councils is to sound out opinions when the board is in process of deciding major changes that may seriously affect the workforce. When the board is considering a substantial new investment (substantial, that is, in relation to the size of the company's resources) or an extensive rationalisation or reorganisation with serious implications for the workers, then it must confer with the council before making its final decision.

As part of a wide review of labour policy carried out in the 1960s and eventually embodied in a series of five Acts, a new company structure was due to come into effect in the Netherlands in July 1973, giving the workers for the first time a strong influence on board appointments. The reorganisation of company structure is based on recognition of the fact that in limited liability companies management has gained independence from the shareholders and acquired a good deal of autonomy. The appointment of a board of directors in large companies has been made obligatory, and the power of the board has been considerably enhanced to provide a counterbalancing authority to that of management in the absence of shareholder pressure. Shareholders and workers will now exert equal influence on board appointments, and the board will in its turn appoint the management and draw up the annual plan for the enterprise.

The method of appointing directors is by co-option. When a vacancy arises in the board, the works council, the management and the shareholders (either at the annual meeting or a committee appointed at it) have the right to nominate candidates. Employee and shareholder representatives have a right of veto over nominations made by the board of directors—if, for example, they do not think the directors' candidate is suitable—but the board has a right to appeal to the Social and Economic Council against the exercise of such a veto. Directors serve four year terms and must then submit themselves for re-election under the same procedure.

This new arrangement will apply to the larger limited liability companies, that is, those which have capital of 10 million guilders, a works council and at least 100 employees in the Netherlands. Private companies which meet these criteria will also have to submit to the same regulations. There are exceptions for international companies. They or their subsidiaries do not have to establish the new-style board, nor, in full, do Dutch international concerns if the majority of their staff and assets are engaged outside the country. It has been estimated that some 400 companies would be brought under the new rules at the start.

Changes in the Dutch law reflect something of the developing attitudes of the Dutch unions. In 1967, the three main union centres (NVV, CNV and NKV) published a joint programme, saying that 'the composition of the board of directors must reflect the interest both of the suppliers of capital and of the workers' and they proposed that equal numbers of shareholder and worker representatives should elect two-thirds of the board between them, and the board members thus elected should themselves choose the remaining third of the board.

Clearly, changes in the law to permit greater worker participation will depend on the attitudes of the workers' principle organisations, the unions, and the pressure they exert. Indeed, there is evidence of a growing demand among union movements in Europe for something like the co-determination system pioneered and evangelised by the DGB.

The reforms in the Norwegian law just described correspond very closely with the demands of the Norwegian LO. The Danish LO has also published a demand for at least one-third of the seats on company boards to go to workers' representatives and for employees also to be represented in the management structure to counteract the growing influence of experts who, the LO claims, increasingly assume the controlling functions of the board. The Swiss and Austrian unions have also claimed reform very much on the German model of parity co-determination. Typically, the Swiss Labour Federation (SGB) argues: 'Co-determination in supervisory boards is of vital importance for the workers, as for the trade unions, because on that level many policy decisions are taken and such decisions should no longer escape the workers' influence.'[16]

In Sweden, the situation has evolved rapidly in recent years. In January 1971, Arne Geijer, president of the Swedish LO, made a speech indicating the unions' hesitant change of attitude. Asking the question, whether it might now be time for the trade unions to take on management functions, he said: 'We have always taken a cautious line in these matters, believing that to be able to assert ourselves both at work and in society at large, the trade union

movement needed not only to be strong, but also free and independent.'[17] In September of that year, LO adopted an action
programme on ways of democratising the company. The emphasis was on enlarging the areas of negotiation. Among the proposals,
the LO wanted unions and works councils to be able to appoint
their own auditors to examine the company's finances and to
participate in planning and budgeting, especially on personnel
matters. It also called for employee representation on company
boards. The LO tried first to negotiate a voluntary arrangement on
worker directors with the employers' organisation, SAF, but
when this failed it turned to the white-collar organisation, TCO,
and together they approached the government. In April 1972
the government published a draft Bill which would give unions
the discretionary right to appoint two directors, and two deputy
directors, to the boards of all companies with more than 100
employees. The Bill became law in April 1973. Moreover, the
Swedish government set up three commissions to study various
aspects of workers' rights. One commission, which was to make
a general review of labour law, was advised to start from the basis
that any new law should replace the traditional employer's right
to hire and fire and to allocate work with a method which gives
the right to decide such matters to both sides working together.
In other words, a broad measure of joint decision on many shop-
floor issues was seen to be the almost inevitable outcome of the
commission's review. The other commissions are also expected to
extend workers' rights, especially over safety.

In Britain, with its traditional emphasis on collective bargaining
rather than on any form of collaborative machinery, it is not
impossible to create methods of consultation that can involve
workers' representatives in participation with management on
important decisions without radically altering the conventional
assumptions of British trade unionists. At the end of 1972, the
coal industry established a joint policy advisory committee 'to
achieve a mutual understanding of problems and to devise common policies to meet them'.[18] Each of the four unions in the
industry could nominate three officials to the committee, while
the National Coal Board (a nationalised enterprise and virtually

the single employer in the industry) would send different members of the board to the committee, depending on what was to be discussed. The committee would be able to co-opt extra members with special knowledge or experience, from outside the industry if necessary, providing that the committee as a whole agreed. Wages and conditions of employment were excluded from discussion in the committee, being left to the existing wage bargaining procedures between the unions and the board.

The collective bargaining tradition and the tradition of institutional machinery laid down from the centre, either by agreement or by law, both have their strengths and weaknesses. The strength of collective bargaining is that it engages the concern of rank and file workers; it cannot work effectively if it does not, because without workers' support trade unions have no sanction with which to counter management authority. And, because it involves workers acting through their unions at every stage, collective bargaining avoids the institutional confusion and overlap that has emerged recently in, among others, France and Italy. But the very sources of the strength of collective bargaining are also the springs of its weaknesses. For, though workers can enforce just as much joint decision-making on management at shop-floor level through the collective bargaining process as can be achieved under any system of laws, the ability to do so depends crucially on a high degree of unionisation. In short, in a country like Britain the exercise of workers' influence is likely to be the result of the accidents of union power. It is no coincidence that the developments in the coal industry described in the previous paragraph followed a prolonged wages strike earlier in the same year and emerged, in effect, from the efforts of the management to put the industry back on its feet by building new bridges with the unions and with its government owners.

The chief defects of pluralist systems that depend on a mixture of union activity and machinery, centrally legislated or negotiated, within an enterprise are the converse of the merits of the collective bargaining process. They have tended to fail to engage workers' interest or enthusiasm; they have weakened union links with their members; and they have dispersed authority among institutions which sometimes conflict. It is too early yet to say whether these defects will be reduced or eliminated following the reforms that have been widespread throughout Europe in the last few years. But this pattern has its advantages, too. It spreads right across the workforce and to some extent insulates workers from the uneven reach of union strength, though if unions are weak it can still be difficult for workers to secure the full advantage of their legal rights. Since under half of the employed workers in most European countries are union members, making workers' rights generally applicable clearly offers important additional protection.

Furthermore, only legal reform offers the opportunity for changes in company structure to let worker representatives join company boards as of right, and thus take part in the formation of company policy rather than, as in the past, merely react to policy once it has been made. On this question, union movements show a spectrum of views. At one extreme, the Italian and French unions are openly hostile to such ideas; the British unions have been sceptical and indifferent, though with British entry to the EEC their attitudes have begun to change; the Swedish unions see workers on company boards as one of many useful additions to worker power but by no means the most important; the Dutch unions give the system their qualified approval, accepting that they should be able to approve the selection of company directors but declining to take part in the direction themselves; and at the other extreme, the German unions are wholeheartedly in favour of workers on boards, complaining only that the system has not yet gone far enough.

As this example suggests, though labour movements everywhere in Europe aim to expand workers' influence and power, they are not by any means agreed on the means of doing so. And there are few signs at present of any convergence of views, even though common trends can be detected.

Notes

Among the principal sources of material in this chapter are:

Papers prepared for a regional joint seminar on Prospects for Labour-Management Co-operation in the enterprise, 24–27 October 1972, Manpower and Social Affairs Directorate, OECD, 1972; *Some Aspects of Workers' Participation*, by C. Asplund, ICFTU, Brussels, 1972; Co-determination: a Contemporary Demand, DGB, Dusseldorf, 1966; Laws against Strikes, Otto Kahn-Freund and Bob Hepple. Fabian Research Series, No. 305, Fabian Society, London, 1972.

1. Kahn-Freund and Hepple, p. 5.
2. Ibid. p. 15.
3. Ibid. p. 5.
4. Ibid. p. 36.
5. Ibid. p. 37.
6. Ibid. p. 13.
7. Ford, C. *Joint Consultation and Co-determination of the Works Councils in Western Europe*, ICFTU, Brussels, 1966. Cited by Asplund, *op. cit.* p. 19.
8. Cited by Asplund, p. 22.
9. Ibid. p. 16.
10. Ibid. p. 16.
11. Ibid. p. 32.
12. DGB, *op. cit.* p. 7.
13. Ibid. p. 7.
14. Ibid. p. 7.
15. Ibid. p. 8.
16. Cited by Asplund, *op. cit.* p. 42.
17. *Industrial Democracy*, Arne Geijer, LO, Stockholm, 1971, p. 5.
18. Joint statement by the management and the unions in the coalmining industry, 21 November 1972, London.

5 Collective Bargaining Under Pressure

For a recent conference in London, the World Auto Councils of the International Metalworkers' Federation prepared a mammoth survey covering wages, working conditions and fringe benefits in forty-seven plants owned by fifteen world-wide motor manufacturing companies. The survey was highly sophisticated—trade unions in three continents co-operated and the results of their enquiries were programmed on the computers of the German engineering union, IB Metall. But its very sophistication made the findings of the survey seem all the more bizarre. It was not just that there were striking variations between continents in the money workers earned—wide differences in pay between North America and Europe are only what one would expect. There were also substantial, and sometimes downright weird, differences between working conditions in the same continent; and not only in the same continent but in the same country; and even in different branches of the same international company in the same country.

In General Motors plants, for example, workers could expect to get forty-six minutes of rest time each day if they worked in the US or Canada, twenty-four minutes if they worked in Great Britain, ten minutes in Germany, and no time at all in four out of six South American countries, the exceptions being Brazil and Venezuela, with five and ten minutes respectively. The British workers, however, could find some compensation in the fact that they got longer lunch breaks than their American colleagues—sixty minutes against thirty. In terms of lunch breaks, indeed, British motor workers seemed to do better than most car workers in Europe, getting sixty minutes also from British Leyland and forty-five from Ford, though admittedly not as well as the fortunate Swiss employees of Volkswagen who were permitted a ruminative ninety minutes.

Overtime rates, too, varied substantially, within a usual range of 125 to 150 per cent of normal hourly pay rates. The full range in fact could be found in Britain alone, with Chrysler paying 125 per cent, British Leyland and General Motors paying 133 per cent for the first two hours and 150 per cent thereafter and Ford paying 150 per cent from the start. Mothers fared differently from country to country. In Britain they got no paid leave from their company in which to have their child; but in the United States and Canada they got forty-two days, in Switzerland thirty and in Germany and Belgium seventy days. For men, marriage did not seem to offer so much. They could take two days off with pay to get married in Switzerland or Belgium, one in Germany but none at all in the United States, Canada, Australia or Britain. Funerals rated higher—three days each in Switzerland, the US, Canada and Belgium, two in Germany and Australia, but again none whatsoever in Britain.

Even within the parent countries of international companies, the survey showed workers at one plant doing considerably better than workers at another. One Volkswagen plant in Germany gave its employees eleven days of paid public holidays a year, while another gave only nine. At three separate plants in Sweden, Volvo gave its workers rest periods of fifteen, thirty-seven and forty-three minutes a day, while in Britain, British Leyland gave ten minutes in one place and twenty in another. On only one point did countries seem more or less agreed: men should not expect to be given leave in which to serve a jail sentence. But even here there were exceptions. In the United States and Canada, jail leave appeared to be common to all major motor companies; and, oddly, British Leyland gave such leave to some of its workers, but not to others; at Longbridge, yes, but at Birmingham, no.

What the International Metalworkers' survey set out to do was to discover what its member unions all over the world had achieved through collective bargaining. Some of the apparently strange differences that were thrown up could be quite easily explained. The companies in Britain that paid no benefits to their expectant-mother employees were not as hard-hearted as they might seem, for in Britain the state provided benefits that were not available elsewhere. The fact that Ford employees in the US and Britain got only their normal wage while on holiday, while those at Ghent in Belgium got twice their regular pay, was no special credit to motor union negotiators in Belgium, since this is now the standard holiday rate for all Belgian workers.

Some differences were not after all as different as they looked; in places where rest periods were short, lunch breaks tended to be long. A close examination of figures can often reveal such balancing factors. French workers, for instance, have had the forty-hour week by law since 1936, while Dutch workers in the engineering industry only got their working week down to $42\frac{1}{2}$ hours in 1970. But in practice the full working weeks of French and Dutch workers are not very different; if anything, the French workers put in more hours than the Dutch—forty-five hours a week against 44.2 on average in 1970.

Other differences are, of course, genuine; others still are merely peculiar. There seems to be no reason why British Leyland should permit some of its workers time off to go to jail and not others.

The message of the survey is that the results of collective bargaining are a combination of many factors of which union strengths and priorities are only one. There are other ingredients just as important—the economic prosperity of the country and the business; the legal and social framework; the interplay of union, employer and state benefits; custom and usage; and even religion, with its influence on public holidays. But, while a detailed survey like the International Metalworkers' seems to throw up a strange hodgepodge of working conditions seen in close-up, standing a little further back it is possible to distinguish some broad trends of development in collective bargaining, at any rate in Europe. It is these trends that will be discussed in this chapter—the changing structure of collective bargaining, the pressures upon it and the new subjects over which bargaining is taking place.

New Pressures on Collective Bargaining

The structure of collective bargaining is being stretched in several directions at once. Under government pressure, national confederations of unions and employers are doing deals of a kind that they did not contemplate in the past, while under pressure from the shop-floor, aspects of which were discussed in the last chapter, unions are also being drawn into new types of negotiation. There is no precisely uniform pattern in Europe, although there are common trends emerging and it is safe to say that in every country dissatisfaction on the shop-floor is causing new problems for unions and employers. The exact stage of development from place to place is, however, the result of the way in which government, employers and unions have chosen to handle certain problems that are common to all.

The regular list of demands that workers now place before employers and governments would have been unthinkable before the Second World War. Then, unions were as much concerned to defend their members from wage cuts and massive unemployment as they were to improve their pay or add to their fringe benefits. Now, the annual claim is as familiar as the annual tax demand. Yearly claims got under way in Britain during the War and in other countries as and when postwar reconstruction was far enough advanced. In France, for instance, the signal was given by the passing of an Act in 1950 aimed at returning to unions and employers rights to determine wages and conditions of work that had been under government control.

At the start, the characteristic bargain was one made centrally between unions and employers' associations. There were variations at local level, but these were minimal. But as full employment became the rule—and in many places labour shortages emerged—centrally negotiated bargains became more difficult to sustain, if only because individual employers were willing to pay more to retain their labour. At the same time workers, sensing the change in the atmosphere, became confident enough to make their own local claims. One way in which to examine the development of collective bargaining is to look at the degree to which national or industry level negotiation has been preserved.

In Britain, the tendency has been very definitely towards abandoning national negotiation in favour of local bargaining. The mark of official approval was given to this trend in a report by the Donovan Commission, published in 1968, which identified the existence of two types of industrial relations system, one formal, consisting of all the official apparatus of the union and its negotiators, the other informal, consisting of the *de facto* appearance on the shop-floor of powerful committees of shop stewards with the ability to make deals on their own account whether their unions or employers liked it or not. The Commission advised that, since the shop stewards were not going to go away, the best thing to do was to come to terms with the facts and to try to re-integrate the two systems by recognising the devolution of power. Another potent boost was given to local bargaining in Britain during the latter part of the 1960s. The government was running a policy of pay restriction in an attempt to reduce the rate of wage inflation, and one of the few ways in which workers could win higher than standard wage increases was to enter into a productivity deal. The essence of such deals was that workers should so change their methods of work—including the abandonment of their restrictive or protective practices—that an increase in output would be possible without any corresponding increase in costs. This meant an attempt to redesign work patterns radically, at any rate in most major industries, which would have been impractical as part of a national bargain. Thus many hundreds of thousands of workers were attracted to making their own, plant-level deals. Even so, national bargaining has not by any means been entirely abandoned. In some industries like coal mining, country-wide negotiation has eliminated previous local differentials and disparities between grades over the last few years; and the two biggest industries in the country in terms of employees, construction and engineering, with one and two million workers respectively, continue to bargain key questions like hours, holidays and minimum rates centrally, though the major part of the actual pay packet and other conditions are negotiated at the building site or the factory.

In Germany, on the other hand, industrial bargaining remains highly centralised, a process which is facilitated by the high degree of organisation on both sides of industry, with only sixteen unions on one side facing a larger number of employers' associations on the other, though it is estimated that these associations cover 90 per cent of firms which themselves employ 95 per cent of the labour force. This strategy appears to suit employers and unions equally well. From the employers' point of view, it helps to eliminate wage competition in an economy so short of labour that up to two million foreign 'guest-workers' have had to be brought in to make up the deficiencies; and from the union point of view, it helps to remove the disparities and inequities between the wages of different groups of workers in the same industry.

Even more highly centralised bargaining over the leading issues of pay and hours take place in the Scandinavian countries. In Sweden the employers' organisation, SAF, has since the Second World War regularly conducted negotiations leading to a basic outline deal with the two main union centres, LO and TCO, which is in force generally for two years, sometimes for one and exceptionally for three years. The hard bargaining is done by three representatives from each side, with about forty delegates of both employers and unions waiting in the background. Negotiations always begin with a thorough rehearsal of economic conditions at home and abroad. Once the outline has been agreed, negotiation is taken up in each sector to turn it into pay deals industry by industry. If, at that level the individual unions and employers' associations cannot agree, a six-man committee of the central organisations decides for them, though it has not often been necessary to refer negotiations back up to the top in this way. The procedure has been slimmed down to some extent by allowing the outline deal to cover some questions, such as pensions and severance pay, in principle only, leaving it to negotiations at industry level to translate the principles into a substantive agreement. In the majority of cases, there is also a third stage of negotiation, over the implementation of the industry deal in the firm.

The procedure is not dissimilar in Denmark. There, under negotiating rules agreed by the employers' organisation, DAF, and the trade union confederation, LO, all agreements must expire at the same time, March 1, while all proposals to amend them must be tabled by the previous October 15. Six representatives of DAF and six from LO meet to consider those questions that are likely to affect every sector covered by an agreement. Out of these central negotiations come the guidelines by which most bargains are set. Affiliates of both sides vote on issues that are centrally agreed; only after this has happened are strikes allowed. As in Germany, centralisation is encouraged by a highly disciplined employers' organisation. The DAF rules say that neither the DAF itself nor member associations, nor individual firms may make agreements with unions without the approval of the DAF general council on: 1. Shortening of working hours; 2. General wage increases (time or piece rate); 3. New minimum wage rates; 4. Holidays; . . . 6. Obligation to employ only organised workers.[1]

In Italy and France, the development of the bargaining structure has been somewhat more complex. While both continue to adhere to forms of national and regional bargaining, other levels of bargaining have begun to emerge. In both countries, indeed, it is possible to date with some precision the moment when local negotiation first became significant. In France, it came in 1953, when Renault concluded a deal with the unions that gave its employees a third week's paid holiday. And in Italy, although there had previously been some local negotiations in industries like building and major firms like Fiat, the important change seems to have come with an agreement in the engineering industry that came into effect in 1963.

But in neither country does the experience of local bargaining seem to have been entirely equable. French employers claim that they simply could not meet the demands of the unions locally on top of the wider deals already made for their industries. In recent years, the trend in the pace-setting engineering industry has been towards a greater degree of centralisation, away from regional towards national bargaining. At the same time, this trend has been offset to some extent by the new rights won in the 1968 Act for union delegates to negotiate in the firm. In Italy, too, the results of the 1963 deal in engineering were not quite what the employers had hoped for. The intention was that disputes in the factory should be referred upwards through negotiating machinery for settlement, and in the meanwhile the unions were to keep the peace. But the unions did not keep the peace, especially after 1969 and, as in

France, the picture was further altered by the 1970 Act which also gave Italian unions new rights in the enterprise. The Italian situation is yet further complicated by the existence of two separate employers' organisations, one for the private and one for the public sector, a split that has existed since 1956. One result of this has been that the procedures in the two sectors in the engineering industry have been quite different. The agreement in the private sector includes a peace clause; but in the public sector, under government pressure, the peace clause was recently abandoned.

Government pressure on collective bargaining has been felt in every country in one way or another (though the most important and common form of pressure, that for wage restraint, will be discussed later and separately). Influence from this direction is nothing new. Governments have generally had a hand in designing the framework within which bargaining takes place. In France, the 1950 Act envisaged two types of deal which are still the basis for negotiations. One was to be between employers and unions and was to affect only the negotiating parties; the other was to be between representatives of the two sides but was to be extended to others in the appropriate industry by government order. The French government also sets a minimum wage rate, *salaire minimum de croissance*, below which no worker may be paid. It is an hourly rate, reviewed whenever the cost of living rises by more than 2 per cent, and otherwise each year in the light of general wage trends; and it acts as a floor upon which other wage deals are built. These are explicit interventions by government. By contrast, in Sweden government pressure on the bargaining framework is implicit. Although earlier legislation had recognised the validity of collective agreements, the present bargaining structure really dates from the 1938 Basic Agreement between the central organisations of unions and employers, which was decisively influenced by government in the sense that it stood ready to legislate if the bargainers could not agree—thus strongly concentrating the minds of both sides—though it did not participate in the negotiations.

The new government influences vary from country to country, according to what are felt to be the needs of the bargaining systems,

though so far, it seems, without any very startling success anywhere. In Britain, successive governments in the late 1960s and
the early 1970s attempted genuinely radical reform. The Industrial
Relations Act which was eventually introduced in 1971 attempted
to formalise union negotiating rights, give government powers to
suspend strike action in emergencies and make collective agreements legally binding. But the early experience with the Act was
not very promising. A railway strike was settled after some of the
emergency procedures had been invoked, though on somewhat
dubious terms from the government's point of view; but the
unions did not exploit any of the Act's possible advantages for
them, preferring instead to take such steps as they could to avoid
the Act altogether and carry on as if it had not been passed. Few,
if any, legally binding collective agreements were signed as a
result of the Act.

Other legal interventions in the bargaining framework do not
appear to have had much better results, at any rate so far as the
peaceful working of the industrial relations system is concerned,
though they have positively enhanced workers' rights. In Italy,
the 1970 Act has tended to undermine collectively agreed procedures by making recourse to the law more attractive to a
worker, who believes he has been unfairly dismissed, than recourse
to any union-employer machinery. If the court finds that he has
been unfairly dismissed, the worker is automatically reinstated,
whereas under an agreement the firm may only be requested to
take him back. The recent French legislation has complicated the
already difficult area of factory negotiation by, in effect, licensing
three distinct but inevitably overlapping types of worker representation—elected shop stewards, appointed trade union delegates
and elected works councils.

The most dramatic legal intervention by government came in
Sweden in 1971, seeming all the more dramatic against the background of the peaceful history of Swedish labour relations. As has
already been said, the Swedish tradition is to keep government
very much at arm's length from the collective bargaining process.
But, in response to strikes and threats of strikes from senior local
government and state employees—including military officers—

the Riksdag passed emergency legislation. The original strikes were on a small scale, only 2,500 state and 3,000 municipal employees, but they were all salaried and some held very senior jobs. The municipalities locked out 5,700 of its employees and the state 28,000, many of the latter in the education sector. More strikes and lockouts followed, but on the day the government was due to lock out 3,000 officers it tabled legislation and all strikes and lockouts were compulsorily brought to an end. The effect of the new Act was to allow the government in the event of strikes or lockouts 'threatening essential civic interests' to order the continuation of the latest collective contract. This the government did for six weeks, and the lockout of military officers was avoided.

Although this dispute (of which more will be heard) was solved, the legislation left the future bargaining rights of public sector employees unclear. The state as employer had got into difficulties with its employees; so the state as guardian of the public had brought in legislation to protect its essential interests. Trade unionists feared that this could allow the government to interfere whenever any action they might take in pursuit of their claims in the public sector was beginning to bite. With comparatively small numbers of salaried employees, the government's strategy worked. But what would happen with a large body of blue-collar workers? So far, this has not been tested in practice.

Other kinds of government intervention in the collective bargaining process have been rather more benign, at least from a union angle. In France particularly, governments have brought pressure to bear on central negotiators to handle a number of social and other questions, sometimes though not usually with the backing of legislation. In 1958 the French National Employers' Federation (CNPF—the *Patronat*) reached agreement with the three main union confederations on an unemployment insurance scheme, to be run jointly. At other times the same central bodies have agreed schemes for payment for short time working and for security of employment. Again, in 1970 the government gave its support to the idea of payment by the month for manual employees, but instead of legally enforcing it employers and unions were encouraged to do their own deals. More compelling were the methods used to introduce General de Gaulle's famous profit-sharing plan. The plan was made compulsory by law, but it was left up to employers and unions to negotiate which of its versions they wanted to operate.

Only one other new pressure on the bargaining structure need be mentioned briefly at this point. It is the increasing importance of the multinational company, which must inevitably have an impact on their host countries. The Ford Motor Company, for example, had for many years an inflexible policy of refusing to join the employers' association in any country in which it built plants. This was at the insistence of the company's founder, Henry Ford I. Although the policy has now been changed, it clearly meant the setting up of a new negotiating system in potential rivalry to the existing national negotiating machinery for the motor or engineering industries in countries like Britain and Germany. In Britain, productivity bargaining got its first real boost through the medium of an international company. Esso compared the number of men required to run one of its oil re-fineries at Fawley, near Southampton, with the manning require-ments of other refineries owned by other national subsidiaries of Standard Oil, its American parent. When it found that many more men were needed in England than elsewhere, because of their craft and other working practices, it initiated the lengthy process of redesigning the work pattern and negotiating its acceptance that was later taken up on a broad scale throughout British industry. Conversely, of course, workers are beginning to think of their employers in a more than national context—to examine, for instance, not merely the profitability of the national subsidiary for which they work, but the profitability of the international combine as a whole. The survey quoted at the beginning of this chapter is an example of this new kind of union awareness of what is happening in countries other than their own, but this develop-ment is so far only in its early stages.

To sum up: the structure of collective bargaining is under stress in every country as new requirements are made of it. Breakdowns have occurred at the upper end of the bargaining scale, as in

Sweden, and on the factory floor in most countries, though perhaps especially in France and Italy. Governments have intervened with legislation in an attempt to repair the bargaining framework, but as yet the results have been inconclusive at best. Central bargaining has been preserved to a large extent in the Scandinavian countries and Germany, but it has shown weaknesses even there and in other countries like Italy it has sometimes looked like breaking down; while in Britain it is virtually official doctrine to encourage plant bargaining. The influence of the multi-national companies has made itself felt, but without a decisive effect on the structure of collective bargaining in any country. There remain sharp differences in the loads that the bargaining systems are asked to bear. The sort of social benefit agreement that has been made in France between the two sides of industry, for example, would in Britain probably be borne by the state social insurance funds. It is perhaps misleading to look for uniform new patterns of bargaining. Structures alter from time to time in every country as new demands make themselves felt in each. Probably the wisest generalisation to make is that bargaining is on the increase at every official and unofficial level in every system, with an intensity that differs from level to level, year to year and place to place. It is to the new subjects of collective bargaining that we now turn.

Demands for Equality

Unions generally express similar ideals of concern for equality for all workers, and not least for women. But the practice frequently falls short of the ideal—because of the economic contexts within which they operate, because of their lack of strength and sometimes because the reality of their intentions is rather different to its verbal expression. If it is difficult to achieve anything like equity in a single country, it is that much more difficult to achieve in Europe as a whole.

The average income per employed person in seven countries in Europe in 1969 has been calculated (in US dollars) as follows: Germany, $3,470; France, $4,176; Italy, $2,812; Belgium, $3,811; Netherlands, $3,987; Luxembourg, $4,037; Great Britain, $2,779.[2] These substantial differences in money incomes, though by no means the whole story of relative standards of living, evidently reflect the wider differences in economic prosperity between the various countries. Nor are these variations static; they are shifting all the time. In July 1971, the British Government issued these figures to demonstrate the percentage changes in real incomes of employed persons between 1958 and 1969 among countries of the then six-member Common Market: Italy, 92 per cent; France, 77 per cent; Netherlands, 74 per cent; Germany, 72 per cent; Belgium, 52 per cent. For the Common Market as a whole the figure was 76 per cent, while for Britain outside the Market it was 39 per cent.[3] Over such trends, the unions have little or no influence, though they can be and often are blamed by public opinion for any shortcomings there may be in their countries' economic performance.

There can, however, be greater equality between the same industries in different countries than between general levels of employment incomes. Printing and publishing is the best paid of all manual jobs in Britain, France and Germany, according to 1970 figures, while coal-mining was either the best or the second best paid in Italy, Belgium and the Netherlands, and petroleum product workers were in the top three groups of well-paid workers in five out of six Common Market countries. Advanced, capital-intensive industries such as petroleum products clearly offer wage opportunities that over-ride purely national circumstances, and traditionally well-organised groups like printers and miners can win high pay in spite of the difficulties and, indeed, decline of their industries.

Even when the law and union aspirations coincide, the results may not be quite up to the standard this would lead one to expect. The Treaty of Rome endorses the principle of equal pay and so therefore do the adherent countries, but women are still not paid as well as men. A sample of metal-working industries in Europe in 1970 showed that women may have hoped to earn as little as 57 per cent or as much as 88 per cent of their male counterparts (a sample for Britain showed a high of 64 per cent and a low of 51 per cent). There have undoubtedly been improvements but it is just as likely that these have come about as a result of employers attempting to woo women out of the home and into jobs in conditions of labour shortage as to have stemmed from union or even legal pressures.

On the other hand, there are some general trends in employment conditions throughout Europe, with advances in one country sometimes having a direct impact on negotiations in another. The success of the German engineering union's drive for the forty-hour week, for instance, significantly boosted the British unions' determination to get the same in the early 1960s. The forty-hour week, though not yet universal, is within sight in most of Europe and the hours actually worked, that is including overtime, are already fairly uniform at somewhere between forty-two and forty-five hours. There is a clear trend in annual holidays too, at any rate in the major industries, where three weeks is now virtually standard and countries like Norway and France are pioneering the fourth week. (In Britain, which has lagged behind in this respect, claims for a third week's holiday were specifically exempted from the legally enforced wage restraint imposed by the government at the beginning of 1973, thus almost certainly ensuring its rapid spread.)

But these are the traditional preoccupations of collective bargaining. Better pay for women and better hours for everyone have been among the objectives of trade unions from the very start—as, it goes without saying, has the simple aim of winning bigger pay packets for all union members. As we have seen, the collective bargaining process has not achieved much in the way of equality either between countries, or between industries in the same country, or between the sexes. But equality is still a bargainers' theme, and it is worth taking a closer look at some of the methods with which collective bargaining has been and is now trying to get to grips with it.

One of the major inequalities in employment is the difference in treatment of blue and white collar workers, the latter being given generous privileges over the former in terms of pay, hours, holidays and security of employment. The old story of the skilled worker of many years' experience who finds he is being less well treated than his eighteen-year-old daughter just out of a secretarial course and into a job at head office still rings true in most of Europe. In recent years a number of responses have developed.

The most straightforward of these are the attempts that have been made to eliminate differences by bringing blue-collar workers' conditions of employment up towards those of the white-collar grades. In France, improvement of the rights of blue-collar workers has been an aim of collective bargaining for many years. Whereas in the past manual workers got public holidays but no pay to cover them as staff employees did, this distinction has been progressively removed over the years. And manual workers have also had extended to them the redundancy and retirement payments that had been normal for staff. There has been a rapid acceleration in this trend since 1969, when the government encouraged industry to equalise terms of employment through negotiations. This led to an agreement on principles between the central organisations of employers and unions which has been turned into practice throughout industry by collective agreements. The main aim has been to give the manual worker, instead of his old weekly pay packet, a monthly pay cheque like any salaried employee (a change known as *mensualisation*). In most industries the change is being made over a three or four year period. Some 80 per cent of French workers were covered by such programmes by the latter part of 1971, with the chemical industry having set the pace by giving their manual and staff employees completely equal status.

In Italy, too, there has been some progress towards *mensualisation*, especially in firms like Italsider and Alfa-Romeo. In Sweden, both legislation and collective bargaining have tended to eliminate old privileges; recent negotiations have been designed to bring the pensions paid by firms to their manual employees, in addition to the social security pensions, up to the standards enjoyed in the past only by staff. In Britain, on the other hand, there has been little attempt formally to eliminate such employment-class differences. The major exception has been the electricity supply industry, which in the course of the 1960s moved its manual employees steadily towards staff status. Unfortunately, the advantages of this were distinctly diminished in the eyes of employees by major redundancy programmes directed at improving efficiency by reducing overmanning and by what was felt to be the failure of management to match their pay, either to the higher standards of productivity to which they had contributed or to the pay deals that were being made in other key fuel industries.

Moving manual workers on to monthly pay has been made easier by the gradual disappearance in many countries of piece rates and other forms of payment related to individual performance. Although in Sweden piece rates still account for some 60 per cent of working time the proportion is diminishing, and in Germany it has been noted that many new forms of work measurement are being introduced, while pay negotiations increasingly ignore performance differentials. In Britain, too, this trend is clear, particularly in the motor industry where the biggest British-owned company, British Leyland, has been engaged for several years in a programme of switching its manual employees from piecework to measured day work (though at a high cost in increased pay) which its chief American rivals, Ford and Chrysler, had adopted years before. Although it has been done to make monthly payment easier, the abandonment of piecework has also had a logic of its own. Modern technology, particularly its scale, has made piecework more and more irrelevant; and piecework systems themselves have shown a tendency to degenerate, so that pay and performance become more and more unrelated, leading to continuous disputes and exercising a ratchet effect on costs. (Conversely, of course, this is why many trade unionists have fought to preserve them, arguing that piecework is more 'democratic' since it may involve constant rate-fixing on the shop-floor rather than, as under hourly-pay schemes, negotiation round some remote bargaining table, and that anyway it produces better results in terms of pay packets.)

Some drawbacks have been identified in the movement away from piecework and towards monthly payment. French employers claim that the extra cost of *mensualisation* can reach up to 15 per cent of firms' labour costs, largely as a result of a rise in absenteeism. And in Germany, where piece and other performance standards have usually been fixed in regional or national negotiations by the unions and employers' associations, new agreements leave these performance differentials to be fixed within the plant. This may weaken links between workers and their unions, since for the German worker the regular union-employer negotiations outside the firm is the main opportunity he has of identifying with his union's activities on his behalf.

Other attempts have been made to remove or reduce inequalities by operating more directly on the wage itself. Here, perhaps, Sweden is the most illuminating example. One aspect of union strategy there has been directed at a common problem: wage drift, or the trend visible everywhere for the wages actually paid by firms to their employees to exceed the levels laid down in agreements. In Sweden, drift is said to account for at least half of workers' annual pay increases—whatever pay increase is agreed through central bargaining is matched, or more than matched, by additions made by individual firms. It has been regular practice for sectors in which drift has been low over the period of a collective agreement to try to make up their regular disadvantage in the next round of bargaining. Attempts have been made to build a mechanism to take account of drift into new agreements, rather than wait until the next agreement and then try to recover lost ground. So, in a two-year agreement, a mid-term point will be fixed. If by then a group of workers have not reached a forecast level of earnings, they will have their pay made up for them. The results of this innovation are so far inconclusive.

This strategy has, however, been in some conflict with another aspect of Swedish union strategy, the absolute reduction of wage differentials. Claims for greater wage equality have been characteristic of LO demands for many years. In 1969, a new approach was tried. Surveys were made in each industry to discover how many workers' earnings were below a certain low level of pay. A fund was then set up based on half the difference between this level and the average earnings of the workers in the industry. The idea was to use this fund to help make up the earnings of the lowest paid. But it quickly ran into a number of difficulties. How was the money in the fund to be distributed—industry by industry, firm by firm, or worker by worker? The LO preferred individual payments, but in the end different solutions were adopted in different industries.

Then there was the problem of existing wage structures. Many of these had been carefully planned and negotiated in order to give an agreed hierarchy of pay related to the familiar criteria of skill and responsibility. If, however, the bottom end of the hierarchy was to be flooded with additional money to be distributed on a quite different basis, that is, of low pay, was there not a danger that the whole structure would be eroded and ultimately made useless? And finally, the scheme came back up against the problem of wage drift. Market forces, it appears, reasserted themselves. Where there was little or no disbursement from the funds for low paid workers, drift was particularly marked. The net result of the 1969 technique for dealing with the worse-off seems to have been little relative improvement in their position, but rather an extra incentive for wage drift and therefore an extra twist to the inflation spiral.

Sweden, as might be expected, is something of a testing-ground for egalitarian ideas about remuneration. As has already been shown, efforts to reduce differentials at the lower end of the earnings scale among manual workers have run into difficulties and the differentials have tended to reappear in spite of anything collective agreements might have laid down to the contrary. But there have also been problems in Sweden at the upper end of the earnings' scale among the very best paid salaried workers. The problem was not so much that of the actual level of salaries, but of the degree of taxation that was exacted from them. Equality was being introduced, not through collective bargaining between union and employer, but through progressive taxation by the state. With the general rise in earnings in Europe, partly inflation-induced, and the increase in government social spending, taxation has become a part of the argument in most wage negotiations, whether for the higher or the lower paid. But the 1971 strikes and lockouts in Sweden which involved senior civil servants and military officers seem to be the first time that high taxes on high incomes have been an important factor in an outburst of militancy by such normally tranquil categories of employee.

A number of other unifying, if not quite equalising, trends may also be noted. The first is for certain bonuses, originally paid only to some members of staff, to spread through the workforce and eventually become embodied in collective agreements or even legislation. Thus in Germany, voluntary Christmas or New Year benefits granted by firms have become embodied in union claims. Subsequently, during the period when the new collectively agreed bonuses are being brought up to the level of the old unilaterally introduced bonus—sometimes the equivalent of a month's pay—the old bonuses may be absorbed into the new collective agreements.

A second trend, or perhaps it would be more accurate to call it fashion, is for wage indexing, or the linking of wage settlements to some outside scale for automatic adjustment in the light of movements on that scale. In a period of inflation, not unexpectedly, union demands are for a link between their members' wages and movements in the cost of living. Wages are commonly linked to rises in the retail price index in Belgium. The anti-inflation deal concluded between the main employer and union bodies in Ireland at the end of 1970 provided in its second phase—to start a year after the deal was signed and to run for six months—a cost of living escalator clause. The deal provided for 4 per cent increases in basic wages and salaries in the second phase; on top of that was to be added a 15p flat rate supplement for every 1 per cent increase over 4 per cent in the consumer price index that occurred during the first year of the deal. The pay increase in the second phase would cover any price rise up to 4 per cent in the first phase, while the supplement would cover any increase in prices beyond 4 per cent.

In Britain, automatic adjustments in pay related to increased prices went out of fashion in the middle 1960s, during one phase of government pay policy, but came back into fashion in the early 1970s, during another phase. The Prices and Incomes Board, set up to monitor the earlier phase, persuaded more than one industry to abandon agreements of this kind, because regular, indeed sometimes monthly, increases in pay rates in line with movements in the price index were judged to do no more than help feed the inflation it was supposed to be protecting workers against, by promoting higher labour costs. In 1971, however, the TUC proposed a new type of linkage, the price threshold. Under this proposal, there would not be month-to-month pay movements according to every point by which the price index rose. Instead there would be a price threshold, say 4 per cent, and only when prices had risen a percentage point above that would increases in wages start to take effect. The government resisted the unions' proposal until, worried by inflation in the second half of 1972, it offered a version of this idea as part of a voluntary package of measures for controlling wages and prices. But the unions liked neither the government's version of its own proposals nor the rest of the government's package and the idea was dropped in the set of compulsory measures put forward by the government in January 1973.

The British unions' proposals were in fact adapted from ideas that had become current in France, especially in the nationalised industries. A variety of formulae had been used in France, but a representative bargain in the public sector was of this kind: the two parties agreed on the real increase in incomes that should be aimed at, say 2 per cent; they then calculated the probable rise in prices over the period of the agreement and made a deal so as to preserve the real increase from the expected price rises. If, however, by the mid-point of the agreement the course of prices was higher than anticipated, the original bargain would be re-opened to accommodate the difference. French negotiators in the public sector have added a further refinement to the concept of wage linkage by introducing a linkage not only with prices but with output as well. These progress contracts (*contrats de progrès*) began in the French nationalised electricity undertaking in 1969 and have since spread to the private sector.

The main aim of such indexing is to remove sources of dispute and tension, in particular to reduce inflationary expectations. The argument behind them is that if workers expect prices to rise in the course of a wage contract, they will naturally make additional claims to cover such rises in advance, and in doing so they will raise labour costs and thus increase the probability that their own worst predictions will be fulfilled; whereas if they know that the value of a smaller claim will be preserved against price rises by linking their pay to the price index, they will be willing to make smaller claims and thus reduce the probability of a high rate of price increase. Economic opinion is, however, divided on whether or not wage indexing acts to fuel inflation or damp it down.

A third unifying point is the increasing tendency towards white-collar unionisation. This is well-established in Sweden, where the salaried and graduate employees' organisations have been considerable bargaining powers for many years. In Germany, the unions have been trying to bring the salaries of senior management within the ambit of negotiations, though with a mixed response so far from employers, and in France collective bargains commonly cover management grades as well as manual workers. In Britain, all the major manual unions have been busy creating or expanding their white-collar sections, while the fastest-growing union over the last decade has been one that caters exclusively for management and other white-collar staffs who have never previously been union members. The motives for this expansion have been mixed. On the one hand, there is the desire of the unions to recruit up the income scale in order to bring more employees within an egalitarian framework of negotiation; or, more crudely, simply to expand their memberships. On the other hand, there is a new realisation among white-collar employees that they are no longer a group who can rely automatically on their privileges. They have seen their pay and their benefits matched and sometimes improved upon by manual workers. And they have seen themselves every bit as vulnerable to takeover and industrial rationalisation. They have therefore wanted the protection of a union just like any other employee. Whether in the long run this will turn out to be a unifying, let alone an equalising, development remains to be seen. The Swedish LO has recently seen its bid to present a common negotiating front with the white-collar organisations decisively rejected.

Opinion is divided, and the evidence indeterminate, on the real trend in equality. On one side of the argument, it is claimed that unions are increasing in membership and power; that as mass democratic organisations they are bound to use their strength to enforce the interests of the majority of their members, who will, virtually by definition, be the lower paid. It is also suggested that governments and legislatures are reinforcing the movement towards equality under similar mass pressures by encouraging and voting for common standards of employment, especially in the area of fringe benefits; and that the result must be a greater degree of employment equality, with, as a by-product, an increasing disincentive to workers to go in for the sort of training that is now necessary to operate the new and more complex technologies.

This interpretation is reflected by German employers, thus:

The attempt to fall back upon areas with lower wage levels no longer pays at the present time. Wage differentials between urban and rural areas, between areas of high population concentration and districts with less industry are constantly narrowing. Apart from this, the collective wage policy has evened out wage differentials between unskilled and highly qualified workers, between young salaried employees and graduate specialists and generally speaking between manual workers and salaried employees. Firms try to react against this levelling tendency by encouraging wider differentials in the actual earnings paid to their own staff. Naturally the trend is on the increase. Apart from material compensation employers endeavour to satisfy the natural urge among their workers to acquire status. They promote certain of their workers to an 'establishment' category with particular advantages or equate them with salaried employees and give them all the rights of that category.[5]

On the other side of the argument, it is said that wage structures are peculiarly invulnerable to attempts to interfere with them; that when structures are reworked in the interests of the lower paid and equality, the old differentials tend to reappear in spite of everything, usually in the form of some 'black market' payment outside the terms of a collective agreement as in the case of wage drift; and that in any case unions are not interested in equality between workers as a whole, only in the sectional advantages they can win for their own members.

The experience of the Swedish experiment in helping the low paid embodied in the 1969 agreement described in this chapter, seems to support this view. In 1972 in Britain, when the government proposed to the unions a flat rate £2 a week increase to all employees as part of its anti-inflation package, it was pointed out that this, if it was accepted, would be the first concerted attempt to interfere in the interests of equality with the structure of earnings in Britain, which in spite of 100 years of continuous trade union activity had remained largely as inequitable as ever.

No doubt there is validity in both arguments. Inequalities persist between the top and bottom of the national wages structure, while within the structure differentials will have been eroded in some industries to the point where there may be serious loss of material incentives for skilled workers. Union structure does not appear to be the mainspring of inequities, as is sometimes thought. At any rate, similar problems arise in the Swedish system, where the unions are highly centralised and organised on an industrial basis, and in the British system, where the unions are highly decentralised and organised in a variety of often competitive ways. Unions will continue to make claims both for greater equality and for larger differentials, and tension between the two types of claim seems likely to be characteristic of collective bargaining into the indefinite future. An alternative would be some sort of comprehensive national job evaluation system, as has been suggested from time to time, but this has been little more than talked about outside authoritarian systems of government and is unlikely to be applied in Western Europe where free collective bargaining has so far been seen as part of the democratic process along with adult suffrage and other liberties.

New Demands or Conditions of Work

While the argument over fairness continues, other demands are beginning to make themselves felt. One of the most important concerns the whole area of working time. Until recently, union claims have tended to be limited to the traditional question of the working week, with the target for most of this century having been set at the eight-hour day and the forty-hour week. Their other main associated area of interest has been the retirement age. Now the forty-hour week has been accomplished, or is within sight, in most of Europe and retirement pensions are paid by the State at age sixty-five to men and sixty to women. With these gains secured, unions are raising their sights to more ambitious targets.

Claims for a thirty-five hour week are already becoming commonplace in Britain, though so far there is little sign of a breakthrough for manual workers. An exception is the electricity supply industry, which at the end of 1972 claimed two hours off their working week in order to bring their hours more closely into line with those of clerical workers and so consolidate their advance towards full staff status. It is probable that the thirty-five-hour week will become the general union target for the late decades of the century as was the forty-hour week for the early decades.

But some workers already set a higher priority on a shorter working life than on a shorter working week. A recent survey in Germany[6] has shown that German workers are more interested in earlier retirement than they are in either fewer hours or longer holidays. The same is reported to be the case with Dutch and French workers. As a first step, optional systems are likely to be operated, so that an employee may retire early on a lower pension or late on a higher pension. In Germany such choices are already possible. A second stage will be demands for a general reduction in the retirement age, which the French CGT and CFDT have already put forward jointly. Along with these claims will be matching claims for better pensions—up to three-quarters of final earnings—'dynamised' so as to take account of increases both in costs and standards of living during workers' longer lives in retirement, and transferable from one job to another. This will be a complex area of negotiation, involving as it necessarily will co-ordination between state pension schemes and employer schemes at a time of labour shortage when firms are not likely to exert themselves to make it easier for their workers to shift to another employer. But the trend towards a shorter working life and improved retirement is certain to be reflected in more and more union claims. European workers are, however, still a long way from the American target of a fixed working life, such as was agreed in a recent General Motors' contract giving employees a $500 a month pension after a straight thirty years' service and making it possible for a man to be retired at fifty or even earlier.

A third new interest in the general area of hours is flexible working time. Conventionally, all employees whether blue- or white-collar have had fixed working hours. They clock in at 8 a.m. and they clock out again eight hours later, allowing for breaks, unless they have an overtime commitment. All workers keep the same hours, though they may be broken down into shifts, and the company's operations are geared to that fact. Recently, however, there have been innovations in the form of flexible working hours. Employees put in the same number of hours at work each week, but they start and finish at times of their own choosing although there has to be a measure of co-operation to ensure that, for instance, an office is not left entirely unmanned. Among other things, this system makes it possible for employees to avoid rush hour traffic if they want and to put in their working hours in fewer days, so that they have a three-day rather than a two-day weekend. There are obvious difficulties in introducing a scheme of this kind for workers in continuous production jobs, like motor car assembly, and pioneering experiments have so far been mainly confined to white-collar employment in, for instance, the Shell Research centres in the Netherlands and some offices in the City of London.

The nature of employees' jobs itself can also be expected to become a subject for collective bargaining. There are signs that this is already happening. Having achieved substantial improvements in their wages and working conditions, and on a wider scale a degree of economic and social emancipation, workers will increasingly question the need for tedious and repetitive jobs. The most famous example to date of this kind of reaction was at a motor assembly plant in Lordstown, Ohio; workers struck, not over familiar grievances of low pay or poor conditions, but simply because the work they were being asked to do was too repetitive and too boring. Such pressure may force employers to redesign jobs so as to remove the tedium from them. The Swedish car manufacturer, Volvo, is experimenting with this in new plant and small experimental projects have been tried by Saab and Fiat. Instead of the process of assembly being broken down into dozens of separate jobs, each one the responsibility of individuals placed at intervals along a moving conveyor belt who have to repeat the same limited and identical task throughout the working day, the jobs are grouped to give each man more variety and more chance to see a significant result from what he does, thus renewing his identification with and interest in his own work.

But these claims can be considered to be still within the traditional ambit of union interest since they are all related to conditions of work, even though the range of claims is expanded to stretch the limits of tradition. Unions are, however, beginning to take a new interest in matters that lie well beyond the limits of tradition. An example of this diversity of interests is this account by Italian shop stewards of their changing attitude to health in the factory:

In the last couple of years, this issue has emerged as one of the most important in all bargaining platforms, and the issue more capable of arousing the fighting instincts of the workers than almost any other . . . From the workers' point of view, this new attitude means first of all refusing extra payment for unhealthy jobs—'we don't sell our health'—substituting this traditional management way of buying off its refusal to eliminate harmful factors with easy cash payments . . . The movement that has developed on this question in the factories in recent years is closely linked to the demand of the trade unions in the country at large for a real national health service, democratically controlled and run, with the power also to enter the factory and demand the vital changes which are urgently needed in the interest of the health of the community.[7]

In Britain in 1972, the unions made their agreement to a government package of wage restraint measures conditional on a whole range of demands being met that strayed well outside the usual limits of union bargaining. These included an immediate increase for old age pensioners, a lower than anticipated level for Value Added Tax when it was introduced a few months later and even improvements in the terms of British entry to the EEC. In the same year, the Dutch unions attempted to go even further. Having negotiated an anti-inflation deal on pay and prices with the employers, they then proposed a social contract to the government. Among their demands were levies to finance housing and pensions, smaller classes in infant and primary schools, a scheme for training young workers, and the withdrawal of government proposals that would have diminished social benefits including the freezing of some family allowances. Dutch workers were willing, in other words, to trade zero or minimum increases in real earnings for social advances. A union official summed up their new attitude: 'We discovered in a survey of our members' opinions last year that our men like to fish and swim in clean water, breathe clean air, be rid of traffic jams and industrial noise. Holland is over populated, over polluted. These issues have become a priority to the extent that wages have taken second place.'[8]

Such environmental and other concerns distant from the unions' traditional sphere are likely to become increasingly important subjects of trade union controversy. And where they cannot be or are not handled by more directly political methods they are sure to be embodied in trade union agendas for collective bargaining.

Workers' Asset Formation

A mixed political and collective bargaining approach by the unions is also probable over the last of the new types of demand that will be discussed in this chapter—what is rather clumsily called workers' asset formation. This is in fact nothing more than a modern version of an ancient union claim, that the ownership of capital is too heavily concentrated among too few people and should be redistributed. Formerly, unions satisfied themselves on this question by calling in their programmes for extensive nationalisation and then leaving it to a future labour-oriented government to give their programmes effect. Calls for national-isation are still heard on union platforms, though less and less. They are being replaced by a new demand, for the socialisation of capital, and the demand is being given new meaning in carefully thought out, detailed schemes for achieving redistribution by placing capital ownership in the hands of workers and their organisations rather than in the hands of the state. Several schemes have already been, or are being, introduced in Europe, though none of them so far fully matches up to trade union ambitions.

The new line of trade union argument is roughly as follows. The ownership of capital in spite of all the changes of the last thirty years, remains the privilege of a few. Thus in Germany it has been calculated that 75 per cent of the country's total private property is in the hands of only 17 per cent of the households.[9] And in Britain it has been estimated that almost a quarter of the total net personal wealth is owned by 1 per cent of the population and that over a half is owned by the richest 9 per cent.[10] The concentration of ownership of stocks and shares parallels concen-tration of the ownership of wealth in general. This concentration in itself justifies redistributive action. But there is a new phenom-enon visible that reinforces that justification and opens up new possibilities for achieving redistribution. For industry now finances its investment, not by going to the market for new capital, but from its own retained earnings. Between 1968 and 1970 such retentions in Britain averaged £2,895 millions, while spending on fixed capital formation averaged £2,830 millions; thus retained earnings more than covered the cost of new investment. The conclusion is drawn:

The myth that our capital growth is dependent upon the savings of numerous small investors cannot be sustained in the face of this sort of evidence. The reality is one of large con-centrations of financial, economic and political power gener-ating their own capital resources by means of regressive pricing policies and able to divert an increasing share of income and wealth to their own purposes as a result . . . Put simply, workers generally have been and are compelled by the existing economic system to make a contribution, either by direct restraint or . . . through higher consumption prices, to the funds available for fixed capital formation. And they do so without having any direct claim whatsoever on the newly created assets. This process of capital accumulation in turn adds to the wealth and power attached to the owners of existing shares to whom the increased values of the new assets accrue.[11]

The latest union thinking derived from this sort of observation is radically different from old ideas of both nationalisation and the spread of share ownership by merely encouraging and sometimes helping workers to buy shares for themselves. Instead, the unions want workers to be given rights of ownership in the new capital that is created through retained earnings. How such a system might work was outlined by Dr Bruno Gleitze, director of the Economic Research Institute of the DGB, in 1970:

> The gross earnings . . . are first reduced by adequate interest or dividends against the capital of their owners to whom they are due as functional income. The balance is divided up between these owners and the workers. Income is therefore broken down into owners' dividends, workers' share or participation (social capital), and a remaining part, which embodies the actual profit. After the introduction of what is termed social capital, a dividend has to be paid also on this part of the revenue.
>
> The social capital portion on principle remains within the undertaking as share capital, owned by an outside fund (Social Capital Fund). Contributions are 'paid' into this fund as a purely formal accountancy operation, and the enterprise concerned will therefore not suffer any loss in its liquidity or investment capacity . . .
>
> The Social Capital Fund converts this capital into capital asset entitlements of the workers, initially as certificates that are only released as and when they represent a certain value,

considered as a genuine capital asset . . . Otherwise it would involve the risk of being consumed instead of built up—although this particular risk cannot be excluded altogether; it is a crucial problem of capital asset formation policy in whatever form this may be practised.[12]

One of the first of such schemes to be embodied in a trade union programme was devised by Georg Leber, leader of the German Construction Workers' Union, in 1964. It proposed a collective agreement under which the employers would contribute 1.5 per cent of their wages' bill to a fund. The contribution could be in cash, or in the form of an interest-bearing loan or a transfer of shares. The fund would be managed like an investment company, but with certain specific objects including the provision of mortgages for construction workers to buy their own houses and the promotion of an orderly flow of building projects. Workers would receive share certificates in the fund according to the amount that had accrued in their name, but these would normally only be exchangeable for cash plus accumulated interest on retirement.

So far, however, reality has fallen far short of trade union ambitions in most countries. In France and Germany legislation has been introduced which, although it will increase workers' savings, will do little to disturb the existing distribution of capital. In Germany, tax concessions have been given to encourage unions and employers to make agreements on savings—the DM 312 and DM 624 Acts—and in France, in an attempt to fulfil the Gaullist dream of ending the conflict between capital and labour, legislation in 1967 compelled employers with more than 100 employees to enter into negotiations with unions, not on whether, but on how to introduce savings schemes based on special worker participation reserves taken from firms' yearly taxable profits. But these are criticised by the unions because they are limited in scope, because they add to firms' costs, because they reduce firms' investment resources and, more generally, because they are seen as a form of compulsory saving of money which might otherwise have gone to the individual worker in his wage packet to do with as he wished. In France the unions are strongly against the Gaullist package, but in Germany the DGB, which has endorsed the Gleitze plan, accepts the DM 624 scheme as a first faltering step in the right direction and the German unions have now negotiated deals with their employers to cover several million workers.

In Britain, a start has been made in studies by the TUC and the Labour Party, but it is in Denmark that the most comprehensive proposals have been put forward by the trade union movement and accepted in principle by the government, which at the end of 1972 was engaged in drafting a version of the Danish LO's plan. In outline, the LO's scheme is this: a fund would be set up into which all employers—both public and private—would pay in the first year the equivalent of 1 per cent of their wage bill, a figure that would rise yearly by a half per cent until it reached 5 per cent. In limited liability companies and co-operatives, contributions would not be paid into the fund but remain as invested capital, in which the fund would have shares. Employee capital would be represented on the boards of companies and at the annual meeting. The fund would be administered by trade union organisations and run by a board of five members, four elected by the unions and one appointed by the state. Employees would be issued with certificates each year representing their entitlement in the fund, but the certificates would not be redeemable for five years unless death or retirement intervened. Redemption value of the shares would be according to the growth in the value of the fund as a whole over the period of the worker's participation in it, thus ensuring an equal return for all workers irrespective of the performance of their own firms or the fact that they are in the kind of employment, such as the civil service, with which no profitability is associated.

There are, of course, dozens of problems associated with these plans. Which employees should be included and which not? Should there be an earnings level above which individuals might be expected to take care of their own capital accumulation? On what common accountancy basis should profit, and the workers' share in it, be treated? How would multi-national enterprises be brought in? Would, indeed, the presence of such mandatory capital-sharing deter multi-national companies from bringing investment to some small countries, as trade unionists in Austria fear? How could the risk that these worker-owned savings would be turned into consumption at the first possible opportunity be avoided? And, since a fund of the type proposed by the Danish LO could quickly turn into the biggest single source of investment in the country, is there not a danger that one concentration of power—in the hands of a minority of individuals—might only give way to another—in the hands of the trade unions?

But the concept is now firmly placed on the agenda of the European unions, rounding out a programme directed at making serious inroads on old employer and owner privileges and it is certain to be a prominent subject of negotiation in the future.

Notes

The most important sources used in this chapter are: *Recent Trends in Collective Bargaining*. Final report and supplement to the final report, OECD, Paris, 1972; *Survey of Collective Bargaining Agreements in the Automobile Industry in North America, Europe and Australasia*, International Metalworkers' Federation, Geneva, 1972; *Accumulation of Assets for the Worker*, Georg Leber, Frankfurt, 1964; *Report on Seminar on Industrial Democracy and Asset Formation*, International Federation of Chemical and General Workers' Unions, Geneva, 1970; *Labour Relations and Employment Conditions in the EEC*, Coventry and District Engineering Employers' Association, Coventry, 1972; *Collective Bargaining and Inequality*, Jim Skinner, Fabian Research Series, No. 298, Fabian Society, London, 1971.

1. Constitution of the Danish Employers' Confederation, cited in *Industrial Relations in the Common Market*, Campbell Balfour, Routledge and Kegan Paul, London, 1972, p. 56.
2. *ECSO Yearbook*, cited by Coventry and District Engineering Employers' Association, *op. cit.* p. 49.
3. Coventry and District Engineering Employers' Association, ibid. p. 48.
4. Ibid. p. 61.

5. Gunther Herzog, director-general of Employers' Association for Rhine Palatinate Neustadt, OECD, seminar, supplement to final report, p. 49.

6. By Infas, quoted in OECD, *op. cit.* p. 133.

7. Statement by Pirelli–Dunlop international steering committee, 1972.

8. Piet Vos, director for economic policies of the industrial group of NVV, quoted in *Sunday Times*, 5 November 1972.

9. Quoted by Leber, *op. cit.* p. 17.

10. Quoted by Skinner, *op. cit.* p. 1.

11. Ibid. p. 3.

12. International Federation of Chemical and General Workers' Unions, *op. cit.* p. 31.

6 *National versus International*

Towards the end of 1972 the Central Committee of the International Metalworkers' Federation met in San Francisco. It was an impressive gathering of trade union leadership from around the world. Ninety delegates represented twenty-four countries from every continent. Among them were the leaders of some of the world's biggest unions outside the communist countries, including Hugh Scanlon of the British Engineering Workers and Leonard Woodcock of the American Automobile Workers. The Federation already represented some 11 million workers, and at that one meeting the committee decided to admit to membership unions in three continents representing another half a million workers.

This is, in part, the account given later in the Federation's own newsletter of a report to the meeting by Daniel Benedict, a Federation assistant general secretary:

IMF action should concentrate on specific multi-national companies such as General Motors, Ford, Chrysler, Toyota, Nissan, Westinghouse, Singer and SKF.

In these companies the IMF would support organisational campaigns, specific educational seminars and promote joint collective bargaining goals. In cases of conflict, letters, cables, talks with world and local management and mobilisation of public opinion should be used. Combined trade union action should take place in all subsidiaries of a given multi-national company. Affiliated unions should educate their militants to use efficient machinery of pressure such as working to rule, 'blacking' (refusal to handle material made by strike workers), refusal to handle transfers and to work overtime, and eventually the organisation of brief work stoppages, and financial solidarity actions. Negotiations with international companies should be sought but if the company refuses to negotiate, the power question arises. Therefore, specific target companies have to be selected as well as attractive causes for common action.[1]

It was a resounding programme of action and on hearing it the managements of some of the world's largest businesses might have had cause to tremble. But it was not, perhaps, the action programme itself that was the most significant thing about the report—the programme, after all, was only a typical set of trade union tactics written on a giant scale. What was significant was the grammar. Unions, the delegates were told, should do this and should do that; they were not told that anyone actually was going to do anything, only that they should; and of course to a large extent unions do not do anything at the international level. Benedict's report to the IMF conference was therefore fully representative of the stage of development that international trade unionism has reached. There is a lot of traffic; there are conferences at which delegates make declarations and proposals; a select few multi-lingual union officials jet around the world with all the weary elan of their corporate counterparts; but so far as most trade unionists are aware, it might never be happening.

Yet the increase in the volume of international union traffic cannot be ignored. Already it has had some influence, at least in shaping international opinion, and even in rare cases in organising concrete action. The noise of this new traffic can be compared to the sound of a swarm of bees. The swarm hovers hesitantly, not yet sure where to land; but when it does it could have a startling effect on those who happen to be in the neighbourhood.

International solidarity has always been one of the themes of trade unionism, and it has always been intermittently displayed. More than 100 years ago, Abraham Lincoln was moved to thank the cotton workers of Lancashire for a boycott of Confederate cotton during the American civil war, even at the expense of their own jobs. And there have been regular international contacts and influences within labour movements from the beginning. As has already been said, Danish trade unionists helped their Swedish colleagues to start their own unions; the example of the first British co-operative at Rochdale was followed within a year in Germany; and the first round of contacts between management and labour in Sweden that ultimately led to the Basic Agreement was inspired by the similar talks that were held in Britain after the 1926 General Strike at the instigation of Sir Alfred Mond. But the early promise was never fulfilled. Probably more than anything else, the nationalist feelings which overwhelmed labour ideals at the outbreak of the First World War destroyed the hopes of European co-operation that had seemed so likely to trade unionists in the years before. In many ways, the trade union movements of Europe are as isolated now as they have ever been.

There are numerous reasons for this, for instance, the political split that has divided unions internationally since communists and non-communists broke apart in 1949, but one problem has been especially important. Where should the focus of international unionism be, supposing an effective international movement could be created? For a national movement, this is no problem. Unions in every country address themselves to the country's business enterprises on some questions and to its government on others. But the equivalents on an international scale are not so easily recognised. In 1972, the world's airline pilots organised strike action in order to call the attention of the United Nations to the spreading threat of hi-jacking, but this was a rare if not a unique case of an international institution existing that had, at least in theory, the power to redress a specific grievance. Such institutions are thin on the ground and not very powerful, as the pilots soon discovered. The International Labour Office (ILO), a UN agency based in Geneva, offers one possible channel for union activity. Here, union officials can help to shape international labour standards; but these scarcely matter unless they are accepted by individual governments and then enforced in practice, so the union leader quickly finds that in order to get things done he has to return to action within his normal sphere—his own country.

In recent years, however, two new sorts of organisation have begun to attract European union interest. The first is the multi-national company and the second the organs of the EEC. These have seemed to offer to trade unionists for the first time a target for action and a possible negotiating partner not unlike those they are used to. The multi-national company is a larger version of the company they do business with at home, and the EEC is a new source of rules and regulations comparable to a national government. Since these are the growth points of international trade unionism, it is with them that this chapter will be concerned.

Multi-National Companies

There is nothing new in the idea of enterprises with operations in more than one country. Nor is there, as yet, much evidence that the characteristic union fear about them—that they will create jobs in another country at the expense of jobs in their own—has much foundation, at any rate in Europe. It is just as likely that jobs will disappear as a result of new patterns of demand, for which the new source of supply happens to be foreign, as has happened throughout Europe to the once-impregnable coal industry; or because industrialising countries can supply goods once manufactured in Europe at a lower price, as has happened in textiles without the intervention of multi-national companies. What is new is the trend to increased size among such companies, to the extent that it is being freely forecast that by the end of the century two or three hundred of them may dominate the economies of the non-communist countries. However that may be, it is a plain fact that their increasing visibility has provoked a union response.

Not surprisingly, the first initiatives have come from America. As the home of the majority of the largest multi-nationals, American trade unions were the first to experience their possible consequences. Between 1968 and 1972, the American electricians' union (IUE) lost 50,000 members, largely as a consequence of the shifting of electronics work such as the manufacture of transistor radios and black and white television sets from the United States to Asia. Similar fears drove American unions into forming inter-nationals and into some of the earliest trans-national bargaining.

The Automobile Workers, with members in both Canada and the United States, made wage parity in motor plants in both countries a negotiating priority, which was finally achieved in 1967. US investment abroad, which the unions saw as likely to reduce job opportunities at home, has led the AFL-CIO to reverse its traditional free trade policy and back restrictive legislation in Congress, aimed at curbing the outward flow of capital and the inward flow of goods. At the same time, it has called on agencies like the ILO to establish fair labour standards, that is, standards which will reduce cost advantages in other countries; and individual unions have taken the lead in establishing and promoting the international trade union secretariats, mainly in Geneva, which link unions with members in the same industries but in different countries.

In Europe, the first response to the multi-nationals came later even though some of the largest of them are European in origin. British experience is not untypical. Early debates at the annual conferences of the TUC, beginning in 1963, concerned the labour practices of foreign-owned companies. They paid sub-standard wages, it was claimed, or they refused to follow usual British practice and recognise trade unions for purposes of negotiation. In 1969, when the phrase multi-national companies started to enjoy currency in union circles, the Chemical Workers' Union introduced a motion that compelled the TUC to take a serious look at the activities of the mult-nationals, and in the following two years its annual *Economic Review* contained sections on them. In 1970, the TUC called a special conference on the subject.

The fears expressed by British trade unionists, and they reflect those of other labour movements, have been distilled as follows:

1. Implications for the job security of British trade unionists.

2. A possibility of resistance to and/or withdrawal of trade union recognition.

3. A change in the balance of power in collective bargaining against the British trade unions.

4. A problem of trying to locate the real source of decision-making in such companies, and

5. A potential conflict between the interests of foreign com-

panies and the interests of the British government in maintaining
the welfare of its citizens.[2]

There is obviously some real substance in each of these arguments. Some American companies pursue a world-wide policy
of not recognising unions, for example, IBM, Kodak and Gillette.
And the obligations on companies that do not have a share quota-
tion in Britain to reveal information about their activities is
limited; thus it is difficult for trade unionists to find out what is
happening and who is ultimately responsible. Yet there is another
side to these questions. There are wholly British companies that
are just as hostile as any other to union recognition and there can
be advantages in ignorance to British unions, who are in any case
disinclined to accept that what they know about a company's
profitability is a limiting factor in their negotiations. (The British
subsidiary of an American-owned oil company had shown a
deficit of several million pounds in their latest accounts. The unions
were in process of putting together a wage claim. I asked the
chairman of the company if he expected his losses to be quoted
in the forthcoming wage negotiations. 'Good Lord, no,' he
said. 'They could always say that group profits were as good as
ever, if they cared to mention it at all.')

A classic incident that aroused all the latent hostilities and
suspicions of the British unions came in 1971. Workers at Ford
company plants staged a ten-week strike over their pay claims.
Henry Ford himself visited Britain at the time and was received
by the Prime Minister as if, commentators observed, he was a
statesman of equal standing. Ford announced that British com-
ponents would no longer be used in overseas assembly plants
and he hinted that there was unlikely to be any new investment in Britain in the near future because of the strike record. Now,
it seemed to trade unionists, the multi-national company was revealed for what it was—powerful, arrogant, able to play off the
workers in one country against the workers in another, able to
subvert national hopes and government plans for new jobs,
almost, indeed, an economic power to rival that of a national
government. But in practice, things did not work out as Henry
Ford's hints had suggested to the unions they might. Towards the

end of the two-year labour contract over the terms of which the 1971 strike had been called, the British Ford company announced record profits and major plans for expansion. Union fears were proved to be empty. Events had shown that a national subsidiary of a multi-national with heavy investments was just as anxious to protect and enlarge its interests as any purely local company would be.

Nevertheless, trade union suspicions of the multi-national company remain. In the long-run, some union leaders believe, they should be subject to regulation on a world basis, in just the same way as national companies are regulated by the laws of the countries in which they are incorporated. In the meantime, working through the international trade union secretariats in Geneva, the unions are just beginning to build up the foundations of a countervailing power on the international scale equivalent to the power that unions created in their own countries years ago.

It is a slow hard grind., The secretariats—the main ones cover printing, agriculture, chemicals, food, metal industries, transport and supervisory work—typically foresee a four-stage programme. First they undertake research, to provide their affiliates around the world with new kinds of bargaining information (the Metal-workers' survey of wages and conditions quoted at the beginning of the last chapter is an example). Then the secretariats try to handle new kinds of problem on an *ad hoc* basis as and when they arise. This amounts to turning the secretariat into a kind of post office. Affiliated unions send in appeals for help and the secretariat officials in turn contact other union affiliates who may be able to put pressure on another, more sensitive, point in the multi-national structure. The secretariats handle many such appeals from unions in developing or authoritarian countries, especially Turkey and Spain, and claim some limited successes. A case in point concerned Peugeot in the Argentine. There was a national motor strike; Peugeot declined to negotiate, sacked eighty men and laid off 1,000 more. The local unions appealed through Geneva to French Peugeot workers. Their protest was taken up by the metalworkers' CFDT affiliate in France, and eventually the Argentinian workers were reinstated and a working party set up to examine the causes of the dispute.

The next step in the secretariats' programme is the co-ordination of bargaining. This is a limited move, involving no more than the arranging for claims against the subsidiaries of one multi-national company in several countries to coincide, but even this is difficult enough to achieve since contract lengths and other aspects of the bargaining timetable vary widely. So far, the unions' most striking success has been with the French-owned St Gobain company in 1969. Unions in four countries—the United States and three countries in Europe—agreed to bargain at the same time and to co-ordinate their actions through a committee under the wing of the International Chemical Workers' Federation in Geneva. The essential point of their agreement was that the unions in each country agreed not to settle their claim with local management before all the others were ready to do the same. This was to make sure that the company could not make up the production it might lose through a strike in one country by increasing production in another country. The unions in each country finally declared themselves satisfied with the offers that had been made to them—and with the tactics that they believed had contributed to the offers being made. Although there have been other cases of union pressure in one place reinforcing union action in another, the St Gobain negotiation in 1969 remains a unique case of co-ordinated bargaining in several countries at once. But even it falls far short of the fourth and final stage of development envisaged by the secretariats—world-wide bargaining on a common programme. So far, there are no recorded examples of this happening.

The progress of these secretariat programmes is inevitably slow. Collective bargaining is still firmly embedded in national frameworks. Unions are largely national, not international, institutions and in this they reflect the feelings of their own members who continue to define their aims and draw up their bargaining targets by reference to standards set in their own national societies. For the time being at least, workers are almost certainly showing good judgement in limiting their attempts at co-operation. A survey made in Canada among Chrysler workers revealed that 53 per cent were prepared to strike in support of Chrysler workers in the United States, but only 10 per cent to back British workers and 9 per cent to back Mexican.[3] This seems to represent a fairly shrewd assessment of where the Canadian workers' own real interests still lie.

But as new economic circumstances emerge, union attitudes change with them. This is already beginning to happen in Europe where a degree of consultation and bargaining has developed in parallel with the development of Europe-wide companies and of economic integration, and European labour institutions have been established to handle the new problems. These are at several levels; confederations that participate in the work of EEC organisations, and industrial committees that represent unions in the same industries in different countries in much the same way as do the international secretariats in Geneva.

The industrial committees—of which the most important cover agriculture, metalworking, transport, building, chemicals, textiles and food—have not yet attempted collective bargaining with the multi-nationals. Indeed, they are on the whole still against the idea, believing that on the central bargaining issues of wages and hours national unions should continue to adhere to national negotiating systems. What they have aimed at instead is discussion and consultation on social questions. The European Metalworkers' Federation, for example, has established working relations with Philips, Continental Can, Brown Boveri and Fokker-VFW. Regular meetings are held between union and management representatives, generally starting with exchanges of information and views, and progressing towards common understandings, though not to collective agreements as such. At the fourth meeting between Philips management and union officials, these were the subjects which the unions tabled: the economic, financial and technical outlook; personnel planning; training and retraining; the establishment of a social fund, out of which displaced workers would be paid their normal wages for a fixed period following redundancy or a change in the location of jobs; and an annual written report on the economic and social development of the company.

This is not collective bargaining but it is squarely within the European tradition of consultation. There has not so far been a collective bargain in Europe between the management of a multi-national enterprise and unions in several countries. The nearest to a bargain of this kind across an industry has come in agriculture. In 1968, after several years of preparation and negotiation, farm workers' leaders and the European Agricultural Producers' Association (COPA) signed an agreement for harmonising the working hours of permanent employees in crop farming. A commission was also set up to prepare a similar agreement covering livestock farming. The crop farming agreement only had the force of a recommendation and was not binding on the farmers of the then six-member Community, but it was the first approach to a conventional collective agreement that had yet been made in Europe. It is not hard to imagine that, as the European community takes shape and the movement towards full monetary and economic integration proceeds, new forms of bargaining will appear, including eventually full-scale collective agreements with the major international companies.

Meanwhile, the pace of *ad hoc* demonstrations of union action in support of unions in other countries can be expected to increase, both within the multi-nationals and more generally. Already there have been examples of both. In 1972, 30,000 shipyard workers in Rotterdam and Amsterdam went on strike for two and a half weeks over a pay claim. Not all the unions with members in the industry were agreed on the strike and the Dutch courts prevented the union that did support it from making strike payments. But member unions of the European Metalworkers' Federation in other countries contrived to make money available to the strikers. In the final settlement, the Dutch union persuaded the employers that these payments were not illegal and it was able to return the money. Later in the same year, joint action by chemical workers in three countries—the Netherlands, Belgium and Germany—forced the international chemical company AKZO to reconsider its decision to close down three plants and dismiss 6,000 workers. There was a brief strike at one factory, in Wüppertal, and the International Chemicalworkers' Federation called on workers in twelve countries to institute an overtime ban. But the key action was the occupation of a plant in the Dutch town of Breda—the first time this had ever happened in the Netherlands —and after four days the company agreed to think again.

The development of joint trade union policy and action towards the multi-nationals within the EEC is, however, likely to be slow. It is not only that trade unionists have not yet felt much need for it; the framework of the EEC as yet does little to encourage it.

The European Economic Community

The European unions took an early and in general favourable view of the building of supra-national institutions after the Second World War, though the communist unions were initially hostile and continue to have strong reservations. As early as 1949, a union conference was called to consider the Allied proposal to establish an international authority to reorganise the coal and steel industries of the Rühr, at which American and British union representatives were also present. But the Allied proposals were quickly overtaken by the plan put forward by Robert Schumann for a European Coal and Steel Community, which was already seen as the first step towards a wider common market and perhaps even a federation. The unions backed the plan and acted to establish their influence in the High Authority which was set up by the treaty signed in Paris in 1951 to run the first of the new communities. Paul Finet, a Belgian trade unionist, was appointed to a seat on the Authority, and at one time no fewer than three seats were filled by men with union experience. The principle result of this strong trade union presence was the introduction of a measure that was at that time a complete innovation: the Community financed the redeployment of workers whose jobs were affected by rationalisation or technical change.

The majority of unions were still in support when the Rome treaties were signed in 1957 creating the European Economic Community and the European Atomic Energy Community, though they had reservations. There was not enough supra-national power and the European Parliament was assigned a minor role. There was no trade unionist among the senior officials of the new institutions—none was appointed until 1967, when Wilhelm Haferkamp of the DGB became one of the Commissioners at Brussels—and, more broadly, the social commitment of the EEC was less than had been that of the Coal and Steel Community.

This last point has been important in determining the scope for trade union interest at EEC level. Although there have been some improvements since 1957 and the promise of a new concern with social questions like regional policy brightened with the Paris summit meeting in 1972 and the enlargement of the Community at the beginning of 1973, the fact remains that the Common Market is still basically what its name suggests—a market. A market is primarily an arrangement to make trading easier and this is reflected in the fact that only a handful of clauses in the EEC treaty reveal any interest in social questions. These deal with such things as equal pay, the free movement of labour, the exchange of young workers and the ultimate harmonisation of social policy. A structure like this clearly has little attraction for trade union activity, except perhaps the attraction of changing the structure. For one thing, it does nothing to promote the chief union interest, collective bargaining, and the bargaining framework as a result remains overwhelmingly national. This is implicit in the way in which the treaty has given labour and capital similar freedom of movement between members, that is freedom for individual workers to change countries in search of new work. But, it has been argued, these are not true equivalents. Capital's rights 'are essentially rights for collectivised, accumulated capital. The logical correlative of a freedom of trans-national movement for "capital" would be a legal right of trans-national, collective bargaining for "labour" '.[4] Bargaining does not, of course, necessarily follow merely legal guidelines but it is certainly influenced by them and the influence of the EEC has been on the whole negative.

The nearest that the unions have come to conventional bargaining activity at the overall European level was the adoption in 1965 of a common action programme by the European Confederation of Free Trade Unions, a group of the major non-communist, non-Christian union centres in the six member countries. The programme had four main points: reduction of working hours to a maximum of forty a week, worked over five days; the extension of holidays to four weeks per year; an improvement in holiday pay from the present rate, that is, normal wages, to double normal wages; and income security, so that workers' living standards are maintained when they are unable to work either through physical incapacity or retirement. At the same time the Confederation created a standing commission for information on wages policy to issue quarterly and annual reports on the development of wage bargaining in the member countries. Although this is not in itself bargaining, the setting of common targets and the circulation of information have helped to shape the direction of union claims, as recent progress on holidays and holiday pay in each country indicates. The Confederation's aim has been to help to create common standards in wages and conditions throughout the Community in much the same way as common standards had been achieved in individual countries, though not itself to be involved in the necessary bargaining.

Apart from this, the unions' main role at Brussels has been to take part in the extensive, though from a union point of view not very satisfactory, system of Community consultation. Such consultation has not been made any easier by the unions' own continuing disunity, which persists in Europe as it does at the national and world-wide level. Three union groupings have set up Brussels offices through which they attempt to influence EEC policy. These are, first, the European Confederation of Free Trade Unions, the European arm of the International Confederation of Free Trade Unions, of which the German DGB has been the largest and most influential member; the European Organisation of the World Council of Labour (formerly the International Federation of Christian Trade Unions), whose most important members are the French CFDT and the Belgian and Dutch Christian unions; and third, the standing committee of the French and Italian Communist union centres, the CGT and the CGIL. The Free Trade Unions were involved with the earliest efforts to establish European institutions, from the Ruhr Authority onwards; the WCL set up a European organisation in 1958, soon after the signing of the Rome treaties, though the communists boycotted the whole enterprise until 1966 when they claimed their share of consultative rights, which they were given three years later. Substantial working co-operation has been achieved between the Free Trade Unions and the World Council of Labour, though the former has kept at arm's length from the communists. This may change with the enlargement of the EEC. The British TUC is cool if not outright hostile to the EEC but it will certainly participate in European union activities in due course, once permanent British membership has become assured. The logical place for the TUC to fit in the Brussels system would be as a part of the Confederation of Free Trade Unions, since the TUC is already affiliated to the ICFTU, the world body of which the Confederation is a regional grouping. But TUC leaders were quick to express their reluctance to join a new lobby from which communists and Christian trade unionists were excluded. As the largest single national union centre in Europe, the TUC could have a decisive effect in changing the structure of union representation in Brussels, and, in fact, when the Community was enlarged in January 1973, the TUC was influential in making sure that the ECFTU was also expanded to take in countries that still remained outside the Community.

Actual consultation is conducted on several levels. For example, trade unionists have the right to meet the chairman before a meeting of the Council of Ministers and they meet the Commissioners three times a year. They are consulted on all major issues either by the appropriate Commissioner or departmental director and they have rights to equal representation with the employers on a number of consultative committees such as those dealing with transport and agriculture. The two major forums for regular union participation are the Economic and Social Committee, set up in 1958, and the Committee for Employment, which began work in 1970. But the unions are in a minority on both and in any case the committees' recommendations are purely advisory. As might be expected from such a slender basis of consultation, the unions' influence on Community policy is small. (An example of the sort of thing they can hope to achieve is the case of tractor design regulations. The unions were asked whether there should be one or two seats on new tractors. Uncertain, union leaders turned to their farmworker affiliates and asked for advice. It turned out there had been a lot of accidents as a result of workers hitching rides by clinging to footholds on one-seat tractors. They therefore recommended two seats and this recommendation was duly accepted. Influence of this kind is obviously something, but not much.) The non-communist unions have therefore called for radical changes in the way the Community operates, including a directly elected European Parliament with real powers, majority decision-making in the Council of Ministers and new consultative bodies of employers and unions within the Commission, with access to all information and the right to initiate policies. As this suggests, the unions are among the most enthusiastic advocates of transforming the EEC so that it becomes a democratic political entity and not merely a market.

But the unions have achieved one important success in influencing Commission policy. When in 1970, the Commission published its proposals for a statute to make possible the creation of European, rather than simply national, companies the thinking behind them clearly reflected the thinking of the Free Trade Union Confederation, and in particular the attitude of the DGB. For it was proposed that a version of the German system of co-determination should be incorporated in the legislation, giving workers board-level rights that had not previously been enjoyed in most enterprises in other member countries. If these proposals are finally accepted by the governments of the enlarged Community, they could have a significant effect on the pattern of labour relations in Europe.

The need for a European company has been felt ever since the EEC began. Since tariff and other barriers to trade between countries were being removed, it was argued, so should the barriers of separate corporate structures which inevitably inhibited cross-frontier investment and industrial rationalisation. Studies were begun in 1964 and turned into proposals in 1970. Existing company structure varied from country to country, but usually joint stock companies had a single level of authority—the board, elected by the shareholders. This conformed with the idea that the company was the possession of its shareholder-owners and thus that they and their representatives alone had the right to make policy decisions. In Germany, and more recently in other European countries like the Netherlands, a new view has taken shape—that others associated with the enterprise, especially the workers, have interests that deserve to be recognised at the decision-making level; in other words, that the enterprise is not merely the property of those who own its capital, but must be shared with those who give their working lives to it. This has led to the concept of a two-level structure of decision, with employees represented in the top tier.

The model proposed by the Free Trade Unions was briefly as follows: a supervisory council which would control the action of the board of directors 'who are exclusively responsible for the management of the firm'. The council would be composed of three equal groups—nominated by the annual shareholder meeting; by 'those trade unions which are representative on the European level'; and by the first two groups as 'representing the interests of the general public'. The unions also proposed a central works council to deal with all the problems that could not be handled by existing local works councils.[5]

The Commission's proposals match the unions' very closely. They include a company-wide works council and a supervisory board. The employees would elect one-third of the board's members, and at least one in three of the employee representatives would be from outside the firm, that is, would not himself be an employee. The supervisory board would choose the management board, of which one member would be assigned as a labour director, and advise it on policy; but the management board would make the decisions and it alone would be entitled to enter into legal commitments. The new works council would be elected proportionately from the component units of the company under the appropriate national rules or legislation. The council would have rights of information at least as great as those of the shareholders and in certain matters like recruitment, training and promotion rights of joint decision with management. Finally, the

Commission's proposals open the way for Europe-wide collective bargaining by empowering the company to make agreements with unions which would be compulsorily applicable to all employees belonging to those unions that sign the agreements.

If this statute is adopted and then made use of by trans-national companies it could have important consequences. For one thing, national legislation will in the long-run be co-ordinated with the Community's, thus changing the corporate structure in member countries to provide employee influence in the boardrooms of national companies; and the existence of international companies obliged to recognise Europe-wide labour institutions and able to make collective agreements is bound to quicken union interest in bargaining on a European scale at other levels, such as that of whole industries.

The first reactions to the Commission's proposals were mixed. Employers' organisations were hostile, as were the communist trade unions; but the Free Trade Unions and those in the World Council of Labour—in the latter case, after some initial hostility—were in favour, as was the Economic Affairs Committee of the European Parliament. Ironically, however, one of the earliest uses made of the Free Trade Unions' scheme in practice appears to have had the effect of actually weakening employee influence. When the German and Dutch steel firms Hoesch and Hoogovens merged in 1972 a new central holding company was created to take over the shares of the two firms and it was decided to establish the new company in the Netherlands, just across the border with Germany. Thus the controlling body of what was now the third largest steel-maker in Europe had escaped the German co-determination laws which lay down parity representation for shareholders and unions on the supervisory boards of coal and steel companies. The new holding company accepted the Free Trade Union proposal for one-third employee representation only, less than the German unions had had when Hoesch was independent.

One step forward and two steps back . . . the road to union power and influence in Europe will be long and crooked.

Notes

1. *International Metalworkers' Federation News*, No. 46, December 1972, Geneva, p. 8.
2. *Multi-National Corporations and British Labour*: a review of attitudes and responses, John Gennard, British-North America Committee, London, 1972, p. 13.
3. David Blake, cited by Gennard, *op. cit.*, p. 48.
4. 'Multi-National Enterprise and Labour Law', by K. W. Wedderburn, *Industrial Law Journal*, Vol. 1, No. 1, March 1972, p. 19.
5. Braun, W., *Free Labour World*, June 1970, cited by C. Asplund, *Some Aspects of Workers Participation*, ICFTU, Brussels, 1972, p. 63.

7 *The Paradox of Incomes Policy*

On 17 January 1973, the British Prime Minister, Mr Edward Heath, held a giant press conference in order to disclose his government's latest plans for dealing with inflation. The setting was impressive—Lancaster House in London—a plush and chandeliered mansion, more often the scene of international diplomacy or the entertainment of distinguished foreign visitors. The plans were bold and elaborate. In the previous summer and autumn months, Mr Heath had tried to persuade unions and industry to co-operate in a voluntary scheme, but the unions had turned him down. He had therefore introduced a 90-day freeze on pay and price increases in November; now he was ready to outline the second, post-freeze, phase of his policy.

Wage rises, he announced, were to be limited to a formula that would allow every group of bargainers £1 a head plus 4 per cent of their previous total wages bill. There was to be a comprehensive system of price control. Special arrangements were promised on sensitive issues like pensions, rents, rates and school meals; the proposals were to be underpinned by legislation setting up a Pay Board and a Prices Commission with powers to enforce the policy.

> 'The whole nation realises that it is essential for the nation as a whole to deal with the problem of inflation,' Mr Heath said tortuously before he described his detailed proposals; and when he had finished doing that: 'And so I believe that these are fair proposals. This is a fair approach . . . that they should continue to have the wholehearted support of the nation in the battle against inflation and that is a battle on which the future of the whole nation depends.'

It all had a fine innovative air about it; the leader of the nation was seen to be trying to muster the energies of the people behind him for a new thrust against that increasingly pervasive and powerful enemy, inflation. But to anyone who had followed these matters over the years, the event was decidedly familiar. Eight years before, in the very same building, a previous government had brought together the leaders of industry and the trade unions to sign a compact on prices and incomes which one minister, in a moment of heady exaltation, had described as being the beginning of the end of the class war itself. But now inflation was running at an even faster rate, and Mr Heath was far from superintending the signature of a treaty with the leadership of organised labour and capital; he was appealing over their heads directly to the people. Since the government had failed to engage the support of the unions, he had little choice.

And indeed, every item in the new package could find a parallel, if not an exact original, not just in Britain but in what had been tried at other times in other countries. The immediate example that had been followed was American. Eighteen months before, another national leader with a conservative, non-interventionist bent, President Nixon, had swallowed his prejudices and launched much the same set of proposals, involving a three-month freeze, a Pay Board and a Price Commission, the expansion of an existing Productivity Commission (matched in Mr Heath's plans by an unnamed agency to help raise productivity among the low paid so as to give scope to raise their earnings) and a system of price control that depended heavily on monitoring manufacturers' and retailers' profit margins. Ironically, when the President had taken his unexpected initiative there had been much traffic in ideas from Britain to America, since in mid-1971 the British had only recently abandoned a system of prices and incomes control following on a change of government and were thus held to be repositories of the latest wisdom on the subject; now the traffic was hastily reversed.

A comprehensive list of precedents could be found in Europe, too, for virtually every detail of the new British policy. As Mr Heath had tried to do, most European countries had at one time or another tried to get union agreement on a package of income restraints; in some of the smaller countries of Northern Europe almost continuously since the Second World War. Mr Heath's original proposal to the unions on pay had been for flat-rate pay increases of £2 a week all round in the interests of giving relatively greater help to the lower-paid within a policy of overall restraint. In Ireland two years before, management and labour had agreed on precisely that pay formula for the first year of an eighteen-month national agreement. Having failed to win the unions round to a voluntary deal, Mr Heath varied the pay formula for his compulsory package. He retained a flat-rate element—£1 a week—but added 4 per cent of each bargaining group's previous wages bill in order to give the unions some scope for negotiations. The Finnish Stabilisation Agreements in the late 1960s followed the same pattern. In 1968, it was decided that the Finnish economy could afford 3–4 per cent pay increases in line with the expected rise in productivity, but the increases were to be given in the flat-rate form of sixteen pennies an hour; and the next year, a second agreement retained the flat-rate increases, raising them to eighteen pennies, but added a further element of 1 per cent, over the distribution of which management and labour would be allowed to bargain. In a White Paper issued at the same time as Mr Heath made his announcement it was declared that 'increases in import costs are a charge on the living standards of all of us which, as a community, we cannot avoid'.[1] In other words, price restrictions would only be applied to goods and services affected by domestic cost increases; higher import prices would have to be passed on to consumers. Elaborate price controls introduced in the Netherlands in 1966 made just the same exception for import prices.

And so one could go on, repeating parallels and precedents both between countries and within the same country. It is hardly surprising that Mr Heath's package looked familiar, for the governments of all Western countries have been faced with similar problems of inflation and, as with other problems of economic management, have had the same limited choice of instruments with which to tackle them. The choice actually made depends on a number of factors—the political complexion of the government, the degree of its public support, the character of its union and employer organisations, the economic situation—but the methods are much the same: only the precise mixture seems to vary. The one thing each country's experience has in common with all the others is that whatever policy is mounted, it appears invariably to run out of steam after a while, leaving the government, usually after a decent interval, to try again with a slightly different, and hopefully more palatable, mixture. At any given moment in time several countries can be guaranteed to be running intensive restraint policies; in mid-1971, for instance, no fewer than seven European countries were operating price and pay restrictions of one kind or another. Britain at the beginning of 1973 was perhaps unique only in the sense that no other major country had experimented with so many variations of policy over the previous decade, only to find that the inflationary problem had grown worse and the sort of popular consensus needed to make the government's policies effective were even more elusive at the end of it all than at the start. But all the evidence suggested that, in spite of all the setbacks they had had, governments were not going to give up trying, in Britain or elsewhere; inflation had not diminished; and unions in every country were going to have to live with the fact that their governments would be making regular attempts to institute incomes policies into the foreseeable future.

The problems to which incomes policies address themselves can be fairly easily defined, if less easily solved. Ever since the end of the Second World War Western governments have been committed to policies of full employment, whether because they thought it morally or ideologically right or merely a vote-catching expedient, or both. In the light of the political disasters that had followed the world-wide depressions and mass unemployment of the 1930s, it seemed in any case only wise. But full employment brought with it hardly-suspected new problems. Labour was no longer the supplicant partner in the economy; it was now heavily in demand. In most European countries labour shortages emerged which had to be filled either from the less prosperous regions of Europe or from the Eastern Mediterranean or Africaro farther afield still. Trade unions did not now need to fight unemployment and wage cuts; they could and did demand constant improvements in their members' wages and conditions. They became, in effect, monopolistic sellers of labour, able to charge more than a 'market price' for their services, thus creating something of a parallel with their employers, whose increasing scale of organisation created positions of market power that enabled them, too, to administer their own price levels. In partnership, then, capital and labour were setting their own prices to their own mutual satisfaction. But they were doing so at the expense of the consumer and at the cost of a general inflation. It is in this process that prices and incomes policies aim to intervene.

Of course there is more to inflation than this (as unions have not been slow to point out). There are droughts and wars and other political events that can pile up shortages or create unexpected demands which inevitably affect price levels; and there are the consequences of uneven rates of growth between countries, changes in commodity prices and the impact of movements in fixed exchange rates. Furthermore, as time goes on, economies adapt themselves to inflation. Cutting the level of demand and raising the level of unemployment no longer exercises the same dampening effect on prices; it may tend to the opposite result as self-confident unions reclaim the reductions in their members' spending power that have been brought about by the very tax increases designed to take some of the pressure out of demand. The amount of unemployment needed to restore the old, gradual rates of inflation grows, and governments are unwilling to take the politically thankless risk of inducing it. They are therefore led to the almost equally thankless course of intervening directly in the wage and price fixing activities of management and unions.

Looked at in the broadest sense, almost any economic activity on the part of government can be considered as part of a prices and incomes policy. If the government cuts tariffs, or promotes a vigorous anti-monopoly programme or stops manufacturers from fixing the prices at which retailers sell their goods, then it is evidently stimulating competition, including, with luck, competitive price cutting. In the same way, if it improves the quality and quantity of training and retraining, or if it introduces special social benefits such as those for redundancy or unemployment, or if it encourages extra growth in depressed areas, or if it presses greater efficiency or productivity bargaining on unions and management, then it is, again with luck, making a more efficient labour market by removing blocks and frictions from it. Clearly, by creating more effective markets, the government is helping to reduce the likelihood of inflation. But, for the moment at any rate, we shall consider the narrower, more direct forms of intervention, those that impinge on management and unions themselves, first by looking at the way policy has developed in several European countries.

The Netherlands

Wages and prices have been closely monitored by the Dutch government since the end of the Second World War. In the first phase, up to 1958, collective agreements to increase wages were subject to statutory approval. General lines of policy were laid down by the Social and Economic Council, a tri-partite body comprising government, union and employer representatives. Agreements had to be approved by the National Board of Mediators. All aspects of wages were liable to checks by the Wage Control Service of the Ministry of Social Affairs, including performance standards and incentive schemes. During this period there was developed an extensive system of job evaluation, leading to the adoption in 1959 of a standardised fourteen-point method of evaluation which has been widely accepted in Dutch industry. Some 70 per cent of manual workers in industry are covered by it, though only 20 per cent of white-collar workers.

In 1959, there was a change of direction. Regular wage rounds were replaced by what was called a 'differentiated' wage policy. The aim was to introduce productivity advances as the main criterion for pay rises. Proposed increases were vetted by the Central Bureau for Statistics in the light of the relevant industry's productivity performance over a period of years. It was hoped that this would provide a basis for a prices policy as well, since wage increases leading to price rises in low productivity sectors were to be balanced by price cuts in sectors of exceptionally high productivity.

Within two years, the new system was seen to be in need of amendment. Consistently higher productivity in some industries than in others was leading to unfair wage disparities; boom conditions meant that in any case employers were willing to pay above the levels justified by productivity alone; and there was felt to be too much checking and vetting of wages by government agencies. So there was another change of direction. Instead of the key criterion for wage increases being the rate of productivity improvement in individual industries, guidance for all industries was to be sought from a wider range of economic indicators, in the shape of norms provided every six months by the Social and Economic Council and endorsed by the government. The power to approve increases was transferred from the National Board of Mediators to the Foundation of Labour, a joint management-union body set up during the war to deal with labour and other matters outside the ambit of the occupying Nazi regulations. But the Board of Mediators and the government retained considerable reserve powers. If the Foundation could not reach agreement on a particular deal, the Board could give or withold its approval; the Board could advise the government to make an above-norm deal non-binding; and the government could impose a wage freeze of up to two months if it thought wages were getting seriously in conflict with other economic objectives. During the freeze the government was to consult unions and management and if it was unable to strike a satisfactory bargain with them it could continue the freeze or put the whole system of wage negotiation back under the aegis of the Board of Mediators.

In spite of the new machinery, wage movements quickly got out of hand. Average pay went up 15 per cent in 1964 and 11 per cent in 1965 (Common Market entry and over-heating of the economy may have been among the reasons for this wage explosion) and the Foundation of Labour was unable to agree a wage policy for 1966. The build-up of wage rises continued—by May 1966 agreements covering more than half-a-million employees and averaging $10\frac{1}{2}$ per cent against a government guideline of 7 per cent were still in the pipeline—and the government duly invoked its reserve powers. A short freeze was decreed, full powers were restored to the Board of Mediators and a system of price controls run by the Ministry of Economic Affairs was introduced.

Maximum wage increases were laid down by the government for 1967 and the employers matched this with an offer of voluntary price control. In the event, the government's wage guidelines were fairly closely observed—perhaps as much because of economic conditions as because of the guidelines themselves—and in 1968 the requirement of government approval for wage agreements was dropped, though the right of government to declare agreements non-binding was retained. A new attempt to consolidate government reserve powers was also made in 1968. Essentially, wage negotiation was to be left in the hands of the bargaining parties but the government would keep the right to declare agreements non-binding, to enforce a general freeze and to return for up to a year to the previous system under which new wage agreements had to be approved. When this policy was spelled out in a parliamentary bill it ran into heavy opposition, not least from the unions. The bill was eventually passed, but several unions withdrew from central consultation with government and employers in protest and they continued their boycott until late 1971 when the government accepted a recommendation from the Social and Economic Council that it should limit its intervention to regular consultation with industry and unions.

In the meantime, the country was left without an effective wage policy. The government tried to meet this situation by imposing a temporary price freeze in April 1969. The Social and Economic Council proposed a ceiling for wage increases of 5 per cent in 1970, as part of a package of anti-inflationary proposals, but a series of strikes in the middle of the year, starting with the Rotterdam dockers, led management and unions centrally to agree a maximum of Fl 400 increase for some workers, a sum that was at once claimed by transport, building and engineering workers. Eventually a series of industry by industry agreements was reached and the strikers returned to work in mid-September.

Britain

In the immediate postwar years the Labour government had the support of the trade unions for a policy of restraint in which wage increases were to be kept in line with the rise in output. No central institutional machinery was required for consultation or wage determination. But the unions withdrew their support from 1950 and for a period governments were largely content to rely on other tools of economic management. In 1957, the Council on Productivity, Prices and Incomes (commonly called the 'three wise men') was set up to 'keep under review changes in prices, productivity and the level of incomes'. Although there was more than one attempt at a form of incomes policy by government exhortation and example, consistent efforts to create a comprehensive policy did not get under way again until the 1960s.

In 1961 the government imposed a 'pause' on wages and dividends against trade union opposition and some restraint was achieved in the public sector. The next year, a 'guiding light' for wage increases was introduced. Pay was to rise by no more than $2\frac{1}{2}$ per cent, the trend rate of productivity increase. The policy was to remain voluntary, but attempts were made to guide public opinion by the establishment of a National Economic Development Council (NEDC), composed of union, employer and government representatives, to keep under review the general development of the economy, including incomes; and a National Incomes Commission (NIC) to examine particular pay claims and settlements in the light of policy. The unions joined the NEDC but refused to co-operate with the NIC, and although the guiding light was raised to $3\frac{1}{4}$ per cent in 1963 it continued to be breached, as it had been at the lower level.

In late 1964 a new Labour government was elected and the search begun for a voluntary policy that was acceptable to the unions. In December of that year, unions joined with employer and government representatives in a broad Statement of Intent; in February 1965, the National Board for Prices and Incomes replaced the National Incomes Commission as the central body for reviewing pay and prices; and two months later the criteria by which movements in pay and prices should be judged were agreed and published. Average wage increases were to be within a 'norm' of $3\frac{1}{2}$ per cent, but a series of exceptions were allowed on such grounds as low pay, productivity and the need to attract new labour. Price guidelines were also set out, again with exceptions, such as the need to attract new capital.

Although the policy and the judgements of the Prices and Incomes Board undoubtedly had some effects, they were limited, and in any case the first voluntary phase of the policy was swept away in the blizzard of a balance of payments crisis in July 1966. The government introduced a series of deflationary measures, including a six-month 'standstill' on prices and incomes to be followed by a period of 'severe restraint'. The standstill was backed by legislation which allowed the government to set aside increases in pay or prices for up to twelve months. The standstill was very successful and the period of severe restraint largely so.

In mid-1967 the restraints were eased slightly. The target for price and income increases remained nil, but exceptional treatment was made easier. The government dropped its main powers to put down price or pay increases, but it retained powers of compulsory notification for proposed increases, coupled with a right to suspend the increases for six months while they were being examined by the Prices and Incomes Board. In 1968 a $3\frac{1}{2}$ per cent ceiling was substituted for the nil norm, though any increase in pay was supposed to be justified on strict criteria, and the reserve delaying power associated with investigations by the Prices and Incomes Board was increased from six to twelve months.

The next year, however, saw a major switch in government policy. Prices and incomes policy was retained—in December a programme for 1970 envisaged a range of pay increases between $2\frac{1}{2}$ and $4\frac{1}{2}$ per cent—but the emphasis was turned towards a reform of the industrial relations system itself. The impetus for this came from growing public concern about strike action, particularly unofficial strikes, and the publication in the previous year of the report of a Royal Commission. Reform was stated by the government to be an essential part of its economic strategy. However, it withdrew its proposals, under pressure from its own parliamentary supporters and from its trade union backers, both of whom were concerned that some of the clauses in the government's bill could lead to the imprisonment of trade unionists, and accepted instead a binding obligation on the part of the TUC to act against unconstitutional and inter-union strikes. From then until the election in June 1970, the façade of an incomes policy was maintained but it was pursued without much enthusiasm.

The new Conservative government elected in 1970 also abstained from pursuing an interventionist incomes policy at first, in order to press its own legislative proposals for industrial relations reform. A wide-ranging Industrial Relations Act was passed in 1971 with the aim of making the conduct of collective bargaining more orderly. But it aroused intense union opposition and in its first year of operation did little to alter the industrial relations atmosphere, except perhaps to embitter it. In the meantime the government pursued an incomes policy of a kind, though it was never articulated or discussed with the unions. This was what came to be called the 'N — 1' policy. Having found the rate of wage settlements running at a high level when it took office, the government tried to use what influence it had with negotiators to make successive settlements lower in percentage terms. This strategy appeared to be having some success, especially in the public sector, but the rate of settlements turned up again in early 1972 following substantial breakthroughs by miners and railwaymen. The government then embarked on a series of discussions with the unions and employers through the summer and autumn of 1972 which it was hoped would lead to a voluntary deal, but the unions rejected the government's proposals and a compulsory freeze was instituted in November, to be succeeded the next year by a rigorous package of price and wage controls (some of the details of which were described at the beginning of this chapter).

Austria

Since the Second World War, Austrian unions and industry have run with a considerable degree of success a series of prices and incomes policies, characterised by mutual agreement and a degree of government participation, though not intervention as is statutory elsewhere. In 1947 the two sides of industry established an Economic Commission to make recommendations to the government on questions of economic development, and one of its first actions was to institute a three-month freeze on wage and price increases. Although in the inflationary conditions of the time this initiative had only a restricted effect, employers and unions were sufficiently encouraged to make four further successive annual agreements. And in 1951 the unions agreed to a pause on their pay claims which lasted for two years while management organisations encouraged businesses to hold or reduce their prices (in some cases achieving price reductions of 5 per cent).

After something of a lull in active incomes policies—perhaps as a result of the very success of the 1951 agreement—there was a resumption of interest in 1957 following an acceleration of the economy and of the rate of price increases. The Economic Commission was replaced by a Parity Commission on which sat representatives of government as well as unions and industry. The Commission, which was modified and reformed in 1962 and 1963, operates stabilisation policies for prices and incomes on a completely voluntary basis, and, with the formation within it of a Council for Economic and Social Questions, it has become a forum for the discussion of basic economic problems and for making recommendations on their handling.

On wages, the Commission works in this way: a trade union that wishes to make a claim first submits it to the national union centre, the Trades Union Federation, which sorts out and aligns wage claims and then passes them on to the Incomes Sub-Committee of the Commission. (Only labour and employer representatives sit on this sub-committee; government is present only at the level of the Commission.) The sub-committee can give the go-ahead for negotiations, or ask for a postponement, or for more information; or it can submit the union proposals to the full Commission. When the negotiation is completed the resulting bargain is again submitted to the sub-committee which may go through the same procedure of approval or deferment. All major pay claims are submitted to the Commission, which also hears every case on which the Incomes Sub-Committee cannot agree.

The sub-committee works on a basis of unanimous voting.

It is claimed for the Austrian system that, at any rate until the early 1970s, it had succeeded in maintaining a rate of growth of about 4 per cent for a decade while keeping a relatively high degree of price stability. Voluntary prices and incomes policy had also been useful in helping to iron out fluctuations in the economy. Thus during a recession in 1967 substantial wage rises were agreed; while in the succeeding upswing the unions were willing to exercise considerable restraint.

Germany

Until the mid-1960s little attempt was made in Germany to run an explicit incomes policy. Uncertainties associated with the return of democracy to the country, the political division between East and West, economic reconstruction and the collective memory of pre- and postwar inflations all combined to create a mood of voluntary restraint on the part of the unions. In 1964, however, the Council of Economic Advisers made a number of suggestions for the development of wages in the economy, and from then the concept of 'concerted action' over wages has grown. But it has never been taken to the point of direct government intervention in the process of wage negotiation. The emphasis has been on the provision of information, joint discussion and the co-ordination of private decisions between employers and unions with general economic trends.

The 1964 Council report simply drew attention to the fact that on the assumption of external and monetary equilibrium, costs would remain stable only if wages rose by no more than the average increase in productivity. It did not propose any rigid norms by which wage negotiators should steer. For instance, it suggested that a certain wage pressure might not be unhelpful in prompting industry to raise its efficiency through programmes of rationalisation. It accepted that in sectors where labour was short, pay increases above standard would be appropriate, while in sectors which were overmanned the opposite should apply.

Incomes policy was given a more specific form in 1967 when the Growth and Stability Law introduced a system of regular forecasting and consultation in a forum that brought together several times a year representatives of the Council, the union and employer organisations, the Bundesbank and the government. The results have been uneven. When it has gone wrong it has not been so much because of union unwillingness to co-operate but because of faulty forecasting.

In the early months of 1967 there were wage reductions. But it was soon agreed that this was unhelpful to economic recovery and so changes in policy were made which in early 1968 were seen to have made 'a significant contribution to . . . more rational decision making'. For the same year, conflicting forecasts of economic growth were made by the government and the Council. The latter proposed an upper limit of $6\frac{1}{2}$ per cent to the increase in GNP, while the former proposed 4 per cent. In the event, unions and employers agreed to stand by the lower, government forecast and agreed to wage and salary increases that fell within the 4 to 5 per cent limits the government thought the economy could accommodate. But as things turned out both sets of forecasts were too gloomy. Real growth rose to a rate of 7 per cent, and union support naturally declined. In 1969 the government set a growth target of $4\frac{1}{2}$ per cent, but again it underestimated economic potential. The economy actually grew by 8 per cent. In the light of what had happened the previous year, the unions gave the government's wage guidelines of $5\frac{1}{2}$ to $6\frac{1}{2}$ per cent little more than nominal support and wage rate agreements averaging $7\frac{1}{2}$ per cent were made in the first half of the year. By the autumn, the economy was manifestly booming. Profits were high and the labour market in a condition of strong excess demand. Germany's first postwar bout of wildcat strikes followed. Employers were compelled to renegotiate wage contracts ahead of time and by the fourth quarter of the year wages and salaries were $12\frac{1}{2}$ per cent higher than they had been twelve months before. Ironically, this meant that the share of wages and salaries in the national income was just about what the Council of Economic Advisers had advised a few years before that it should be. Since then government, unions and employers have found it more difficult to agree on either overall economic policy or wage guidelines, and wage settlements have run at a rate considerably higher than the growth of productivity.

There are certain common features in most attempts to run an incomes policy, as these examples have shown. For instance, every country seems to have felt the need for a top-level consultative forum bringing together the leaders of the unions, industry and government, and backed up by common research and information services. Sometimes this forum proves to be all that is needed, as in the case of Germany; more often, it has to be buttressed by more extensive machinery like the Prices and Incomes Board and later the Pay Board and the Price Commission in Britain, the Incomes Sub-Committee of the Parity Commission in Austria and the Board of Mediators in the Netherlands. The content of policies, too, shows regular similarities. In each country, norms for annual wage increases associated with rises in productivity make an early appearance in the formation of policy, though by themselves such norms are usually soon found to be an inadequate measure.

The precise shape of incomes policies depends on the character of the institutions in each country, particularly its labour organisations. Where a broad consensus exists between the unions and government on the objectives of economic policy, an elaborate system of incomes control may not be necessary. This was the case in Britain in the first five postwar years when a tacit understanding between union leaders and the Labour government existed and the government needed to add to that little more than moral exhortation directed at the public at large. In Germany, the postwar consensus between government and unions has survived more completely than elsewhere as unions continue to give price stability an over-riding priority, and the formal complexities of a full-blooded incomes policy have scarcely been necessary. In Italy and France, on the other hand, agreement between the leading trade unions and government hardly exists even on the structure of democratic society, let alone economic policy or the shareout of wages within the national income. Thus governments have, not surprisingly, been reluctant to embark on the always difficult task of seeking union support for explicit policies of wage limitation.

Perhaps the most familiar identification marks of incomes policies are the signs of their failure. These are much the same everywhere—wildcat strikes, breakaway unions, shop-floor militancy, 'black market' wages and persistent wage drift. As often as not these breakdowns arise from governments and unions, however well-intentioned, selling workers what turns out to be a false prospectus. In Britain in the mid-1960s faster economic growth was promised in return for wage restraint, but balance of payments' crises seemed to defer the promised growth indefinitely and workers' confidence in the policy was severely damaged, a fact which was to be reflected in later union attitudes. In Germany, by contrast, the mistake was in underestimating growth prospects, but the effect on union attitudes was a comparable, if less serious, increase in scepticism about the value and the practicability of incomes policies themselves.

One of the most remarkable things about incomes policies is the difficulty governments have in winning public understanding for them in spite of persistent attempts to propagandise and explain. It has proved to be one thing to persuade union and industry leaders, on the basis of information about aggregates within the economy as a whole, that wages cannot rise faster than a certain rate without damaging other elements in the economy, elements like price stability and full employment that are as much cherished by workers as bigger pay packets; but it is another matter altogether to persuade groups of workers that restraint on their part will be in their own interests, as indeed it may not be, at any rate in the short run.

Investigations[2] in Britain and Ireland have helped to show just how wide is the gap in understanding between policy-makers and people. In January 1971, 37 per cent of those questioned in a British survey could not give a valid meaning to the word 'inflation', while 19 per cent had no more than a vague notion of what it meant. Only 16 per cent appeared to be aware of the relationship between rising wages and higher prices, while 28 per cent saw no connection between pay claims and price rises. An earlier survey taken at the beginning of 1966 when the Labour government had already been making intensive efforts for more than a year to win popular support for an incomes policy, showed that only some 9 per cent of the sample had a fair idea of the policy's aims while 66 per cent seemed to have little or no idea.

The facts of inflation themselves do not seem to be understood; in an inflationary climate, people find it hard to distinguish which goods have risen in price and which have not.

> ... in the February (1966) survey some people said that the price of milk had gone up although the price index for milk had shown a drop of five points. Following price-rises of four points in the spring, the price index for meat and meat products went down by three points before the December survey, and yet a sizeable number of respondents said that meat prices had gone up unreasonably. Likewise a few people mentioned butter as having gone up unreasonably during the [Labour government's 1966 pay] freeze, although the price of butter had gone down in March and then remained the same. Falls in prices which had occurred during the freeze appeared to have escaped the notice of the majority of respondents; when asked whether they had noticed any price decreases only a small minority gave an affirmative answer, with some of them mentioning meat and meat products.[3]

Two other points from these surveys may be worth noting. The first is that while long-term incomes policies were barely understood, short-term emergency action of the kind the Labour government in Britain undertook in 1966, when price and wage increases were frozen for six months, got across to the public much more clearly.

> The terms 'prices freeze' and 'pay freeze'... were found to present no problems of communication, and there was practically no difficulty in getting people to express their opinions on the freeze. Not only was the freeze understood; the government appeared to have succeeded in conveying

some awareness of the need for action. The importance of some of the economic problems facing the country had been communicated to the majority of the sample although a sizeable minority appeared to have no idea of what it was about. About two-thirds of the individuals who saw a purpose in the freeze explained that the country was in debt, the economy was in a mess, the economy had to be put back on its feet; other people were more specific, mentioning the need to deal with inflation, with the wage-price spiral, with productivity or the adverse balance of payments.[4]

The second point worth noting is the range of attitudes towards stable incomes the surveys revealed. Two-thirds of those surveyed in 1966 indicated that they would be content with their present incomes if prices remained steady. The disposition to be satisfied with what they had, provided it was proof against inflation, was more marked in the older respondents. Among those aged 18-19, however, only 41 per cent indicated satisfaction with their present incomes and among those between 20 and 29 years, only just over 50 per cent. Although dissatisfaction among the young is hardly surprising, the survey evidence does seem to suggest that the rising generations are unlikely to be satisfied with an incomes policy that has as its only objective price stability.

Ignorance about incomes policies could arguably be considered the better part of wisdom. At any rate a certain scepticism about them is justified by the record of their success. One test, taking the rate of increase in unit labour costs in a dozen European countries as a measure, showed the following average annual percentage increases between 1953 and 1969: France, 4.2; Netherlands, 3.8; Denmark, 3.6; Finland, 3.4; Norway, 3.2; United Kingdom, 3.2; Ireland, 2.7; Sweden, 2.6; Austria, 2.4; Western Germany, 2.3; Italy, 2.1; Belgium, 1.5.[5] This has been commented on as follows:

The list is headed by France, where no one would claim that co-ordinated incomes policies have exercised a strong influence, but also by the Netherlands, where a complex and —for much of the time—well-accepted, apparatus for executing incomes policy has been in effect. The Nordic countries, with their highly centralised pay bargaining, share the middle positions with the United Kingdom with its highly decentralised system subject only in the later years to a formal mechanism of co-ordination. The three lowest positions—with the smallest increase in unit labour costs—are held by countries without incomes policies.[6]

In other words, as an instrument of economic management to combat inflation, incomes policies have had results that are at best no better than ambiguous. Of course, such tests are by no means conclusive. There are external causes of inflation that are beyond the reach of a country's own anti-inflationary policies, and small countries may be particularly susceptible to such influences (indeed, they may have no wish to resist pressures that keep their own costs in line with those of their larger trading partners). The mere fact that a country has chosen to deploy the full machinery of an incomes policy suggests that it may have peculiarly difficult internal forces to contain—a powerful and militant trade union movement, for example. It is impossible to say what the record of those countries which have managed to combine comprehensive incomes policies with a high rate of inflation would have been like if they had had no policy at all.

Whatever the results have been to date, though, it seems certain that incomes policies are here to stay. In countries like Britain and the Netherlands, where governments have intervened regularly over the years in the processes of wage negotiation, it is difficult to imagine governments abstaining altogether in the future. For a British government to declare that it had no incomes policy—no freeze, no guiding light, no norms, no Prices and Incomes Board, nothing at all—would paradoxically be an incomes policy of a kind all the same, since it would be regarded by the unions as an invitation to lodge very large pay claims and by management as signalling that the government would prefer them to concede rather than resist, even if it meant higher prices. This is just what happened during the last period in which a British government refrained from trying to influence wage negotiations, the months from October 1964 to April 1965, when a new Labour administration deliberately stood aside from the bargaining round while it tried to secure a long-term understanding with the unions.

Government interest in pay settlements is assured, if only because of the increasing scale of employment everywhere in the public sector. Many jobs in this sector, especially in welfare services and administration, do not lend themselves to any easily measured system of rewards, such as productivity or the simple ability to pay, which can be operated by private industry; and governments have to make sure that their own employees are adequately paid by comparison with those in other work. Thus in France, where little attempt has been made to organise a concerted incomes policy, several elements familiar from incomes policy experience in other countries have been built into recent agreements in the nationalised industries. In 1969 and 1970, the French gas and electricity supply industries reached agreements that included a formula for fixing pay which embraced both the industries' own productivity and the increase in national production; in coal mining, allowance has been made for retrospective wage increases to be paid if national output rises by more than a given amount; and in several agreements a price 'threshold' clause has been included, giving extra pay rises if the cost of living goes up by more than a predicted amount.

One other feature common to almost all incomes policies needs to be stressed: control over prices and other forms of income than wages and salaries. In the pay and prices codes published in Britain in early 1973, the government paid elaborate and detailed attention to the non-wage side of its policy equation. Careful distinctions were drawn between those prices that could be raised and those that could not. Imported foods were to be left to follow world prices, but manufactured foods were not; cost increases could be reflected in higher prices, but only if they had been incurred after a certain date and not in full if they were the result of pay rises; sales of second-hand goods were not in general subject to control, but the sale of used motor cars was, and so on. If anything, these aspects of the anti-inflation package were more rigorously handled than wages themselves.

This approach does not imply that governments no longer consider rising wages and salaries the chief engine of inflation that they have to tame. It means rather that they are aware of the need to act on prices in order to demonstrate to the unions that they alone are not bearing inequitably the burden of control; that government is doing what it can to defeat inflation by acting directly on prices; and that the sacrifice of negotiating freedom that unions are being asked to make is being matched by sacrifice on the part of those earning other types of income—so that every group is seen to be holding back from maximising its own income according to its strength in the economy, not just the unions and their members. The importance of making incomes policies comprehensive has been known for many years, but the will to translate this into practice has been slow in developing.

It is this aspect of incomes policy that seems likely to grow in significance in the future. So far, such policies have tended to be used as short-term instruments of economic management. Because they are extremely difficult to introduce, involving official intrusion into previously private areas of decision-making by large and powerful organisations, governments have been reluctant to try except in periods of crisis. A crisis atmosphere can be helpful in persuading public opinion to accept severe restrictions for a limited period—as the success of wage and price freezes in Britain has shown—but such goodwill is quickly dissipated. Long-term policies have been put aside in the interests of the short term. Attempts at reform of institutional structures, improvements in the bargaining framework and the development of productivity policies have, amongst others, been swept aside by immediate pressures. Governments have as a result been apt to find that, after several years of repeated efforts to construct incomes policies, they are no nearer to building a solid foundation for an enduring solution, and perhaps further away than ever.

There is, I believe, at least one important reason why successive incomes policies may become more rather than less difficult—a reason springing from the actual operation of the policies. In the absence of government interest in the outcome of wage bargaining, employers and unions negotiate in comparative isolation. They settle their differences within fairly limited perspectives— the prosperity of the industry and a number of traditional comparisons with pay in other similar or associated occupations. And, providing the negotiators avoid a strike with a damaging impact on the public, the negotiations are not likely to arouse a great deal of interest on the outside. But it is a different matter when collective bargaining is hedged about with agreed or imposed restrictions. Then any wage negotiation, however small the number of employees it covers, may provoke intense scrutiny and wide publicity in the press. At the same time the machinery set up by government to monitor the working of the policy—Pay Board or Parity Commission or whatever it may be—will be investigating particular or general policy problems and then publishing its findings. The effect of all this is to enlarge the framework of reference within which bargaining is conducted. Trade unions may no longer be willing to accept traditional comparisons with a narrow range of other groups. Their bargaining strategy will become more ambitious and their claims more sophisticated. The whole machinery of analysis and investigation set up to support a programme of restraints will paradoxically help to open up new horizons for union negotiators that will make the objectives of incomes policy that much harder to achieve.

A good example of how this can happen is provided by the use of percentages for setting general wage norms. Governments seem typically to start a wage policy by proposing that, since output per head is expected to rise by no more than, say, 4 per cent, earned incomes should rise by no more than the same amount if prices are to stay steady. They then go on to suggest that all pay bargains should be settled within a 4 per cent ceiling, allowing for exceptions in some special cases. It is hinted that the 4 per cent ceiling not only makes good economic sense, it is also equitable because everyone will be treated the same. This may work for a while, but it soon becomes clear that percentage settlements are equitable only in a limited sense: a 4 per cent increase on weekly earnings of £100 is far from being equal to 4 per cent on £20. The demand then grows for a different formula to be used. Hence the recent proposals in Finland and Britain for a standard, flat-rate increase expressed in cash terms, to be paid to every employee irrespective of his present earnings; and in the Netherlands, the insistence by the unions in early 1973 that an agreed percentage should be added to the total wage bill of each sector for the year, then divided equally among all employees in the sector.

Bargaining broadens out in many other ways as a result of incomes policy. When unions confront employers with claims on behalf of workers in an industry or a craft there is not much they can do except to press for improvements in pay and conditions and a narrow band of fringe benefits; a union cannot, for instance, win tax concessions from private industry. But when government invites a national union centre to make a comprehensive pact with it, negotiation takes on an entirely different character. The unions are, in effect, being asked to consider the division of the national income, something which was completely beyond the reach of conventional collective bargaining and which has consequently remained undisturbed for decades. From then on, almost nothing is outside the potential scope of negotiations—taxes, prices, dividends, social security benefits, pensions, housing, even aspects of foreign policy. Government intervention in collective bargaining looks to the unions at first as a restriction on their freedom that must be opposed; later, it may appear to them as an astonishing expansion of their bargaining opportunities.

In the Netherlands, the three main union groups have already adopted a joint programme that specifically recognises the need to limit the increase in incomes so as to provide more resources for social purposes. Their agreement states:

The trade union movement is prepared to accept the consequences of the choice made in the programme, that is, a further rise in collective provisions. This means a moderation in the annual rise of real freely spendable wages.

In this way, room is made by workers for an improvement in the sphere of housing, education, recreation, aid towards development, environmental hygiene, regional development etc. The trade union movement assumes here that the remaining income groups will also make a contribution to the costs of the improved level of provisions.

The burdens of these must naturally be distributed according to the ability to bear them. Accordingly the financing of the wishes in the programme must also be seen in the light of the efforts towards a better distribution of income.[7]

The Dutch unions reached their first agreements on the basis of this programme at the start of 1973. The package covered limitations on wage and price rises for 1973, and it also included clauses on pensions, education and housing. The unions did not get all they asked for and they suffered some internal tensions. The industrial section of the Socialist NVV wanted more far-reaching income redistribution, while conversely the NCHV, representing senior executives, disliked the erosion of income differentials that the package contained and were driven to consider strike action. But the deal marked a clear advance for the unions in the evolution of collective bargaining, and the pressures of incomes policy—the need felt by employers and government to make a deal—gave them their chance.

At the same time as the Dutch unions were concluding their deal, the British unions were reaching breakdown in their negotiations with the government. But the striking thing about the British situation was not the failure but the nearness the negotiations came to success. When the Conservative government came to power in June 1970, it made little effort to propitiate the unions. On the contrary, it pursued a number of policies to which it knew the unions were opposed. It introduced an Industrial Relations Act, designed to reform the framework of collective bargaining, against extreme union protests; it agreed terms of entry to the Common Market which the unions thought unacceptable; and it legislated to raise public housing rents. It displayed an attitude to industrial failure and redundancy which the unions felt to be harsh and therefore deplored. And it ran a form of incomes policy without consulting the unions, which relied heavily on the government as employer resisting large wage claims in the public sector and which the unions thought grossly unfair. In short, the

Conservatives started off with conservative policies, which the unions held to be nothing less than reactionary. But the threat of rising inflation, not to mention its own rising unpopularity, forced the Government to go back on many of its original plans. It proposed unprecedented supports for industry and new aids for depressed regions of the country; an extensive system of control over prices; a variety of safeguards for pensioners, householders and families on low incomes; and a decisive attack on slow growth and high unemployment.

In the event the talks failed—mainly on the issues of Common Market entry, rents and the Industrial Relations Act—and the government moved from attempting to secure an agreed voluntary policy to a unilateral, legally imposed system of price and wage controls. But the failure seems less important than the attempt. A government initially hostile to the whole idea of interventionist controls had reversed its attitudes in an astonishingly short space of time and genuinely tried to gain the support of the trade union movement. Now both the main political parties were committed to achieving as soon as possible some form of voluntary joint economic management with the unions, implying as part of the deal a new social contract. Although the first results of the Conservative's failure to win over the unions were an increase in industrial conflict, the unions had undoubtedly seen the long-term prospect of a whole new area of negotiation open up before them; and it seemed unlikely that any future British government would fail to offer them a partnership in the making of economic decisions.

This chapter began with a statement by Mr Heath; it ends with another, made to the British unions on 2 November, 1972, shortly before the incomes policy talks with the TUC and the Confederation of British Industry broke down. Mr Heath said:

In these talks we have been discussing issues which affected prices and incomes and the relationships between the two. These are matters with which all three of us are concerned. Certain other matters which have been raised are essentially matters of Government responsibility. On these matters the

Government is responsible to Parliament, just as on other matters the CBI and TUC are responsible to their members. These are what might be called policy matters, such as accession to the European Community; the introduction of a fair rents system (a system which we inherited from the previous administration); the Industrial Relations Act; and so on. In these discussions we can take account of the effects of these policies on the issues we are considering; but they are matters of Government policy.[8]

Here, Mr Heath attempted to draw a line across which the unions could not step. On one side were those questions which the government was willing to discuss and negotiate with them; on the other side were questions that were strictly the government's own preserve, over which the unions could hope to claim no influence. In the event it was precisely over those questions that lay on the far side of Mr Heath's line that the negotiations reached a deadlock. But the unions could reasonably observe that Mr Heath had already travelled a long way from his original position to meet them; and they were entitled to wonder whether his, or another, administration might not go further at some later date.

This is surely the ultimate promise of incomes policies for the unions in every country: that their own power to disrupt the economy through untrammelled wage negotiation will compel governments to admit their influence in a far wider spectrum of social and economic policy-making than traditional methods of collective bargaining ever envisaged.

Notes

For the background of incomes policies the following sources have been principally used in this chapter: *Inflation: the Present Problem*, Report by the Secretary General of OECD, OECD, Paris, December 1972; *Present Policies Against Inflation*: Report by Working Party No. 4 of the OECD Economic Policy Committee, OECD, Paris, June 1971; *An Incomes Policy for Britain*, Frank Blackaby, ed., Heinemann Educational Books, London, 1972.

1. *The Programme for Controlling Inflation: The Second Stage*, Cmnd. 5205, HMSO, London, January 1973, p. 4.

2. 'Public Acceptability and a Workable Incomes Policy', Hilde Behrend, in Blackaby, *op. cit.*, pp. 187–214.

3. Ibid., p. 193.

4. Ibid., pp. 194–5.

5. Cited by Blackaby, ibid., p. 220.

6. 'Incomes Policies—What are They an Instrument For?' *Economic Planning and Macroeconomic Policy*, Japan Economic Research Centre, April 1971, para. 29, cited by Blackaby, ibid., p. 218.

7. Quoted in *The Times*, 19 February, 1973.

8. From the official press notice, issued from No. 10 Downing Street, London.

8 *Agenda for Labour*

Several years ago a very senior British trade union official was talking at a party. He was attempting to explain to a group of guests why a strike over pay by some of his members was perfectly justified, even though it had begun well before their existing pay deal was due to expire and in spite of the fact that it had not been officially authorised by the union, 'You see,' he said, 'an agreement is only an agreement so long as the parties to it agree.' He beamed with satisfaction. But the guests were not persuaded; neither was I. What he said then seemed either meaningless or tautologous or simply a reflection of the disorderly state of industrial relations in Britain and the impossibility of doing a deal with a British union. Now, it looks far more like a simple statement of the plain truth; not about Britain but about industrial relations throughout Western Europe.

For every European country has witnessed a wholly unexpected disruption of some kind in the ordinary behaviour of its working people and their unions. The disruption has been more or less dramatic, more or less violent and more or less persistent, but no country has escaped altogether. The result has been to leave the managers—in government, in industry, in the unions themselves—puzzled and more than a little apprehensive. They could not be sure that their conventional proposals would any longer be acceptable, that any collective bargain they entered into would endure. At the beginning of the 1970s, industrial relations everywhere seemed to be in a highly volatile condition.

It all looked very different twenty-five years before. Then, Western Europe was in the throes of reconstruction. War, occupation and a bitter peace combined to soften the divisions within industry. It was not then laughable to imagine that the common purpose of rebuilding a decent prosperity should over-ride the old preoccupations of class and politics, of wages and profits. The trade unions were united as never before. In the Netherlands, before liberation, the unions that had been and still were divided by religion and politics met and agreed rules for future co-operation; they would not, for instance, charge competitive dues in order to win over each other's members; a Council of Trade Union Centres was already in existence when the Allies arrived. The General Confederation of Italian Labour, uniting all the pre-Fascist religious and political tendencies within the union movement, came into being in 1944. In every country, too, co-operative institutions were set up at the level of the enterprise or the factory —works councils, joint production committees, they had a dozen names. Their existence seemed to acknowledge for the first time that a worker was more than a pair of hands or a factor of production; he had something to contribute to the running of his industry, and he had rights inside the factory as well as outside it. The unions were not directly involved in them and the works councils did not negotiate wages and conditions. But it did not at the time seem absurd for the labour movement to endorse them or to subscribe to their purposes—'through co-operation to work for the most efficient production possible and for the well-being of everybody working in the undertaking' (the Norwegian formula, but the others were much the same). Nor, in those early postwar days when work and production were at a premium, did it seem outrageous for trade unions to refrain from using the strength they now had to exact higher wages to the fullest extent of their bargaining power. With or without formal machinery for wage control, union movements as a whole held back.

Such national solidarities did not last. Perhaps they were inappropriate for peacetime 'normality'. Certainly the trade unions were not alone, or even primarily, to blame. If they gave up the austere, moral, united attitudes of the late 1940s, so too did their employers to an even greater extent. It is difficult to trace precisely the process of disintegration or explain why it happened, but some indication can be given of the stages in which the disintegration took place.

Political unity was the first casualty of peace. When the coalition governments of de Gaulle in France and de Gasperi in Italy broke up, the unions' united front went with them. The Communists re-established their own union movements in both countries and there began a series of dizzying political turns and twists, especially in Italy, which equalled that of the political parties. The result was to leave each country with three trade union centres, founded respectively in communism, democratic socialism and Christianity. The political divisions among the European unions were confirmed with the establishment in 1949 of rival internationals, the Communist World Federation of Trade Unions with its headquarters in Prague and the broadly social democratic International Confederation of Free Trade Unions, based in Brussels. The Christian unions, too, contributed to the disarray. In the Netherlands, the Catholic bishops caused a temporary breach in the common solidarity of the Catholic, Protestant and socialist unions, and even for a while excluded Catholics from membership of the socialist NVV. And the Christian unions maintained their own international, the World Council of Labour. But specifically Christian trade unionism declined as a force after the war; their organisations survived but secularisation turned them often towards a nebulous if militant socialism.

The new institutions of co-operation were a second casualty of peace. They were not abandoned; but they revealed themselves as inadequate for resolving the tensions of a more prosperous, more complicated, more divided world. Workers in the factory made demands which the works councils and the joint production committees had no remit to handle and for which the unions were too remote and too scantily equipped. Collaboration—the whole theme of working together—was one thing when employer and employee really did face the same food rations, the same housing shortages, the common need to get things back on their feet; but it was quite another when the problem was one of sharing out an increasing national income.

In Britain, workers simply transferred their interest to the activities of their elected shop stewards' committees, though the system formally survived. In the Scandinavian countries, in Germany, in the Netherlands, in Italy and France, at various times from the early 1960s onwards the system was discovered to be defective and in need of reform. By 1969 an OECD report was able to pinpoint the end of an era of co-operation: 'No matter how works councils have been conceived—as complementary to collective bargaining, or as a permanent problem-solving institution—in Western European industry they have been a failure. The socialist objective of making them an agent of control over management has not been achieved. The Catholic and Protestant objective of satisfying the workers' basic needs of self-determination has not been achieved either. In most countries, workers' reactions to the councils are overwhelmingly negative.' The reason: their 'complete lack of decision-making power'.

The third area of unmistakable breakdown was over incomes. It can never be easy to restrain powerful unions from the exercise of their power. But in the late 1940s the unions had no experience of demanding and getting regular pay rises and in the climate of the times it was perhaps not difficult to persuade them that there was little point in demanding large increases when there were manifestly few goods to spend the money on. Twenty years later, when supermarkets bulged with a huge range of goods and consumer durables poured off the production lines, such appeals for restraint were far less convincing. Consensus survived longer in some countries than in others, and the consequences of its breakdown were more or less serious from place to place. In Britain, the voluntary restraint exercised by the leading unions without any formal machinery was abandoned in the early 1950s; in the Netherlands, a highly complex system of wage monitoring was swept away in a deluge of pay demands at the end of the same decade. In Germany, the unions were exceptionally conscious of the dangers of inflation, having experienced it in its most acute form both before and after the War, and they remained cautious in their claim-making for longer than most other union movements, though even here there was an explosion of wage demands in the late 1960s. But whatever the individual record of each country, the common record of Europe throughout the 1960s was to be one of a bewildering variety of expedients as governments tried first one and then another way of stemming the flood of inflation. Prices and Incomes Boards, Parity Commissions, Boards of Mediators, all came and went as they plugged a breach in the dam, only to come unstuck as the flood gathered new forces. By 1970, no fewer than seven European governments were running explicit policies of intervention in wage and price fixing; the others were resting from the struggle or intervening by stealth.

The end of the postwar era of co-operation was foreshadowed by the erosion of political unity, of the co-operative institutions and of the consensus on incomes, but it was dramatically signalled in the major European countries by a series of incidents which varied in form and intensity and arose from a variety of immediate causes. In France, the break came with the 'events' of May 1968 which, in the French tradition, amounted almost to insurrection; in Italy, there was a paralysing outbreak of strikes in the 'hot autumn' of the following year; in Germany, wildcat strikes were widespread in 1969 for the first time since the war as workers defied management and even their own unions in a bid to win their share from an unexpected economic boom; in Sweden, the government had to resort to snap legislation in 1971 to order back to work senior public servants, including military officers, in dispute over what they saw as narrowing pay differentials; and in Britain, a sullen union movement watched as the strike figures climbed through the late 1960s and early 1970s, largely in protest at government interference in the framework of collective bargaining and at government attempts to limit pay rises, culminating in the decision to call a day of action in the spring of 1973, the first time the unions had undertaken industrial action on such a scale since 1926.

These events alerted public opinion to the notion that something was wrong. But even before they happened movements toward reform had begun to take shape. In the Netherlands, the government established a state committee to review industrial law in 1960; the committee made its report in 1964; the Social and Economic Council then began a five-year study; and the government finally introduced a series of five Acts in 1970 and 1971. In 1965, the British government set up a Royal Commission which reported three years later; in 1969 one British government attempted to introduce reforming legislation; and in 1971 another British government finally managed to pass an Industrial Relations Act. In Sweden, the government set up three commissions in the early 1970s to study labour law—especially that covering collective agreements—and job security and the working environment; and in April 1972 it issued the draft of what seemed likely to be the first of a set of new laws. And apart from legislation there were major reform agreements between national employer and union organisations in such countries as Italy, France and Norway from the mid-1960s.

It is too early to evaluate much of this reform, though some can already be seen to be less than an overwhelming success. However good the intentions of the legislators and the negotiators the means of change that have been adopted have often been awkward in conception and clumsy in execution. In both France and Italy, recent changes have tended to muddle rather than clarify the system of worker representation in factories, so that in France, for example, there are now three overlapping systems —elected shop stewards, works councils and union delegates. And in Britain the Industrial Relations Act of 1971 was so constructed that unions preferred to boycott it almost completely. Although there were undoubtedly some benefits for them in the Act, such as the new rights to be recognised by employers and to have negotiations with them, the unions felt that the Act's disadvantages, like the new right to set up competing unions to challenge existing ones, far outweighed the advantages.

But in spite of these false starts, the general thrust of reform, both voluntary and legislative, was clear. It was to reorganise the channels of worker representation in such a way as to enhance workers' rights and to reintegrate the trade unions with the shop-floor institutions that had been created either by law, by negotiation or by chance. It is worth looking a little closer at how this was being attempted, and indeed why it was needed.

Response to New Demands from the Shop-Floor

In the early postwar period, the characteristic activity of the trade union was the central wage negotiation made annually for a whole industry. This was in itself a novelty—few, if any, unions could previously rely on being able to make an annual wage claim; action against wage cuts and high unemployment were a more likely preoccupation. For this comparatively limited purpose it was not too difficult for a union to carry its members' assent. But full employment brought new problems. A large part of the wage packet was now being determined in the factory; even in a country with a tradition of highly centralised wage bargaining like Sweden, some 50 per cent of increased earnings were being settled outside the scope of the national wage bargain. Added to that, the years of prosperity and full employment had given workers a sense of emancipation and self-confidence, and had encouraged a willingness and an ability to demand new rights over hiring and firing, promotion, methods of production and many more matters that had in the past been the prerogative of management. The trade unions were not capable of handling their members' new, more intimate, demands, and in some cases they were prevented from doing so by laws that kept them outside the factory gates, as in France, Italy and Germany. The works councils were not equipped to do the job either; their role was to consult, not to bargain. The British Royal Commission summed up the problem bluntly in 1968: 'Britain has two systems of industrial relations. The one is the formal system embodied in the official institutions. The other is the informal system created by the actual behaviour of trade unions and employers' associations, of managers, shop stewards and workers.' By then, there was something of this duality in the industrial relations' system of every country. Thus one requirement of reform was to build strong institutions at the grassroots which would not conflict with other, higher-level institutions and channels of negotiation.

The means chosen in each country naturally varied according to the nature of the existing system. The planners might have wanted to start again—to rebuild the institutions from scratch— but they had no alternative except to begin with what was already there. In Britain, the traditional way of resolving problems was in face to face negotiation between unions and employers, from the union leadership that negotiated a framework of pay and other conditions with a federation of employers on behalf of two million workers, right down to the shop steward who argued with the foreman the case of a single worker facing a minor disciplinary penalty. The tradition accommodated a minimum of outside intervention. It was therefore on this basis that new legislation tried to build. In return for a degree of official supervision of their rules by a government-appointed registrar, the unions were to be given new rights to recruit and negotiate and so to extend their membership and increase the range of their influence. The establishment of a works committee system was encouraged, but only as an option that the two sides might choose to adopt and not as a substitute for union-employer negotiation.

In a country like Germany with a well-established institutional system, on the other hand, the problem was rather one of reconstituting the legal institutions to fit new circumstances. The works councils through which relations in the factory were regulated had two defects from the point of view of workers: they were consultative bodies, enjoined to keep the peace, and they were formally kept quite separate from the trade unions. Attempts to remedy these defects were made in the 1972 legislation. Union officials were given rights of access to the factories for which previously they had had to seek management permission, and unions were given certain other opportunities to make their presence felt—for example, by putting forward the first list of candidates for election to a newly established works council. At the same time, the councils were given new powers of joint decision with management, amounting in some cases to a veto on unilateral management action. For instance, management now needed council consent to changes in working hours and breaks, measurement of workers' performance and methods of making payments. The council acquired the right to object to plans for redundancy, hiring and transfers, with a final appeal from either side to an independent labour court.

As the Dutch legislation explicitly recognised, and as the German and British reforms implied, workers in the factory were no longer satisfied with a system which allowed them only a consultative role: the fact that there were conflicting interests had to be accepted and the means of resolving the conflict created. Whatever the method, this was the fundamental purpose of factory-level reform.

But however effective the reform of shop-floor institutions might be, it still gave workers little more than an extension of their previous rights. At this level, even of joint decision-making, it was still a question of management proposing and workers responding. Unions and works council could make a tactical riposte to management plans; they could even persuade management to modify, revise, or postpone changes in working methods, major closures, transfers of work or programmes for hiring, firing or promotion. At best the workers' representatives could hope to exercise a limited right of veto over decisions that had already been made in principle. What they could not do, even with the most fully articulated system of shop-floor power, was to help shape the making of the strategic decisions. But these were becoming crucial. The nature, the timing and the location of investment—it was on such questions as these that the value and the security of workers' jobs were increasingly coming to depend in a world of capital intensive industry where even the largest companies were not immune to the hazards of takeover, rationalisation and bankruptcy.

If workers had a voice and power on the shop-floor, they were starting to want the same things in the boardroom. Only there could they share in the making of the strategic decisions that would eventually be turned into the detailed plans which in turn would determine the pay and the jobs of each individual worker. In the early postwar days, the means to democratic control of industry was often seen by unions to be by way of the traditional socialist technique of state takeover or nationalisation. In many countries substantial sectors of the economy were taken into public ownership—most frequently, the major public utilities such as power supply or transport. But over the years this was discovered to be no panacea. Workers were just as likely to come into dispute with the managements of nationalised industries over their pay as were those in the private sector—sometimes more likely when the government in whom ownership was now vested was trying to run a policy of wage restraint, or when the nationalised assets were in an inexorably declining sector like coal or the railways, as they so often were. Furthermore, whatever advances were made in public ownership, private capital continued to predominate; private employers still provided most jobs.

Two new types of answer were sought to the traditional union concern with the power of ownership and management. One was the dispersal of ownership among a much larger number of people; another was the dilution of management authority through the representation of workpeople in the direction of companies, by putting workers on company boards.

Worker participation of this kind is not by any means a new idea. It was written into the new Italian constitution, though it has not in fact been implemented in Italy. In practice, Germany has probably done most of the pioneering. German companies were the first to have workers installed on their supervisory boards, and German trade unions have set the pace with proposals for the dispersal of ownership, though other countries have plans to outstrip Germany in this respect, notably Denmark.

Variations on this strategy have since been taken up both in trade union programmes and in legislative practice. In Norway from 1973 large companies were obliged to establish factory councils—one-third of its member employees—which would choose the board. In the same year, legislation in the Netherlands gave works councils the right to nominate new board members and, in certain circumstances, to veto the appointment of board nominations from either the shareholders or the existing board members. And in Sweden in 1973 legislation was introduced to allow two members to the boards of companies employing 100 or more workers. In Denmark, Switzerland, Austria and Britain the union movements have all adopted similar policies.

The methods of selecting workers' representatives and the degree to which workers actually want to take on the responsibilities of management differ from one country to another. In Britain, for example, the trade unions insist that only trade union members should sit on company boards; in Germany, workers generally reach the board by way of election through the works council, and need not be union members at all. Again, in Germany the unions demand an extension of their rights so that workers can have equal representation with shareholders on the supervisory boards of all companies, while in the Netherlands the unions at present seek to do no more than ensure that the board has the confidence of the workers in the enterprise. But whatever the means and however developed the ambitions of the different union movements may be, there is at least a minimum of common purpose in these changes in programmes and in practice: to secure for workers more rights and more influence at the highest level of company decision-making.

As yet the second union answer to the traditional prerogatives of capital—the wider dispersal of ownership—has met with a less satisfactory fate. What the unions are looking for is an alternative to the familiar solutions of socialist nationalisation on the one hand and the liberal-conservative concept of wider share ownership on the other. Their proposals start from the fact that much, if not most, new investment is financed from companies' own retained earnings, and they argue that, since workers have contributed to this process of capital accumulation, they must be entitled to rights in its ownership. As has been said: '. . . workers generally have been and are compelled by the existing economic system to make a contribution, either by direct restraint or . . . through higher consumption prices, to the funds available for fixed capital formation. And they do so without having any direct claim whatsoever on the newly created assets.' But in practice union ambitions in this respect are far from being fulfilled, or even approached. In Britain, Germany and France, for instance, legislation has been introduced to facilitate the wider ownership of capital; but only by way of tax incentives to savings, either in the workers' own company or in special funds. This may be of benefit both to the economy and to individual workers, but it does little to diminish the overall concentration of wealth. Only in Denmark, where a scheme for such dispersal drawn up by the trade unions has been accepted in principle by the government, are there any signs that the unions' real target is in sight. Nevertheless, proposals of this kind are now firmly on the union agenda.

Workers' new ambitions were also being embodied in a host of new demands that were added to the conventional shopping list of union claims and began to transform the content of collective bargaining. The ancient union preoccupation with the central questions of more pay for fewer hours worked still continued—the forty-hour week, for example, was formally agreed in France as early as 1936, but it did not work its way fully across Europe until the mid-1970s—and it seemed likely that these would remain the bedrock of union activity. But the basic themes were being broadened out into new forms that the trade unionists of an earlier generation would scarcely have recognised. The demand for the forty-hour week was by the 1970s being turned into claims for a thirty-five-hour week. Two weeks' annual holiday had become the minimum for most workers; now three weeks was in sight as a standard and the fourth week was by no means rare. In Belgium it was already normal, and coupled with double pay for the holiday month. New targets were being set, too, for a shorter working life. Retirement on pension for men at sixty-five and for women at sixty was now general; the next aim was to reduce these figures by five years. In the meantime, a first step was already being taken in countries like Germany, where it was becoming possible to choose earlier retirement at a lower pension or later retirement at a higher pension. The first moves were also being made towards ending the tyranny of the factory clock, by introducing the concept of flexible working hours which allowed workers greater choice in their starting and stopping times. And unions were beginning to challenge, for almost the first time, not merely the pay and conditions attached to work, but the very content of the job itself. A new and less docile generation was starting to question the need for boring, repetitive, assembly line work, and it was showing its dissatisfaction by, for instance, abandoning much of the motor industry to immigrant labour in spite of the high pay it offered. This dissatisfaction was forcing manufacturers from all over Europe to study the experimental plants pioneered by firms like Saab, Fiat and Volvo, in which monotonous, isolated jobs were regrouped to give every worker a chance to do more than a single task and to see something more for his work than a handful of identical bolts tightened into place.

Unions also continued to press for another traditional objective —greater equality of earnings and status. One means of moving in that direction was enjoying a certain success by the early 1970s: the removal of differences in the terms of employment enjoyed by white- and blue-collar workers, for long marked by inequitable distinctions in such matters as security, pensions, holidays, sick pay and methods of payment. In France, the government actively encouraged unions and employers to eliminate such differences and, as one example, by 1971 some 80 per cent of manual workers were getting the monthly pay cheques that had until then been the prerogative of staff employees.

But equality proved easier to talk about than to achieve. Equal pay for women had for years been a union objective and it was being increasingly backed by governments. Legislation set 1975 as the date when it should be achieved in Britain—though only in the incomplete form of equal pay for 'equal' work—and it was one of the social targets of the Treaty of Rome. There had been some movement towards equality; but it was just as likely that this derived from employers' eagerness to woo women back on to a tight labour market as it was to represent the fruits of union struggle, or even of the law.

Even in Sweden, where efforts to achieve a greater degree of equality of earnings among workers have probably had a longer history of concerted union support than in any other European country, it had proved far from simple. In 1969 a new tactic was adopted. Industries were surveyed to discover the spread of earnings and funds were set up to distribute extra cash to those at the bottom of the scale. But this ran up against two snags: the existence of pay structures designed to create incentives for skill and efficiency, which the funds eroded; and wage drift, which operated precisely to offset the distribution of the funds.

Furthermore, the egalitarian trend which the existence of mass trade unions naturally tended to promote, seemed also to provoke its own backlash. One sign of this was the growth of white-collar trade unionism, which now reached into quite new areas of recruitment like finance and the middle ranks of management. In Britain during the 1960s the fastest-growing union multiplied almost ten times in a decade; significantly, it catered for supervisory staffs and it grew largely by picking up groups of them who had never been organised in unions before. The aim of such unions as this was not merely to represent their members to the employers; it was also to prevent the elimination of their traditional advantages over manual workers. At the end of 1972, the Dutch executives' union, NCHV, considered strike action for the first time because of the insistence of blue-collar unions that pay increases for the following year should not be more generous towards managements than workers. And in 1971, the wave of strikes and lockouts that induced the Swedish government to bring in special legislation arose from the fears of senior government employees, including military officers, that their pay differentials were being nibbled away by a combination of higher pay for junior categories of employee and steeply progressive taxation. Did these things indicate that the egalitarian trend had limits? It was too soon to say. But tensions between the demand for equality and the counter-claim for differentials seemed certain to occupy a large part of union interest into the foreseeable future. No final compromise was in sight.

Transnationalism

In the 1960s another new dimension began to be added to union thinking—transnationalism. Unions had always been interested in what happened to their brother organisations in other countries and the international solidarity of workers was an article of faith to most union movements. It was also, from time to time, turned into practice, as when the Danish unions set up a special department to help Swedish labour organise at the beginning of the century. The non-communist unions in Europe were among the most enthusiastic promoters of schemes for building the European Communities after the Second World War, and they remain among the most devoted exponents of the European ideal.

But union idealism was not enough to withstand the passionate nationalism aroused by the First World War; and the actual shape taken by the new European institutions after the Second World War was not of the kind that could engage a great deal of the unions' practical interest. The first of the Communities, for Coal and Steel, seemed a promising precedent. Trade unionists were represented on the High Authority from the start in 1951 and their presence contributed strongly to its policy of financing the redeployment of redundant workers—at the time, an important breakthrough. The Economic Community was, however, less socially sensitive. The social clauses of the Treaty of Rome were few—free movement of labour, equal pay, the sometime harmonisation of social policy—and their effect limited. No trade unionist was appointed a commissioner until 1967. At Brussels, the unions were assigned a merely consultative role. The non-communist unions remained enthusiasts for a genuinely united Europe, but while they lobbied their governments to that end, their day to day practical work was inevitably confined to their own countries. Since the war in many ways the unions have been as inward-looking, as preoccupied with national affairs, as they have ever been, and perhaps more so.

In the 1960s, however, the unions began to become aware of something new—the development of international business. There was, of course, nothing new about capital investment across frontiers. What was different was the growth of the multi-national corporations. Ford, General Motors, IBM, Unilever, Shell—the emblems of the great international firms rose above offices and manufacturing plants in every country in Europe. Their ubiquitous presence provided a focus for union interest; an identifiable, common employer had appeared on the international scene, something equivalent to the national company unions everywhere were used to dealing with.

The unions' response to the multi-national was hesitant and uncertain. In Britain, for instance, they were inclined to speak somewhat chauvinistically about 'foreign owned' companies at the beginning of the 1960s and it was not until 1969 that the more neutral term 'multi-national' gained any sort of currency inside the movement. Nor were the unions quite sure what to make of these companies. Were they just to be feared, because they might transfer jobs from one country to another or offset the effects of a strike in one national subsidiary by stepping up production elsewhere? Or were they possible bargaining partners, to be dealt with by international alliances of trade unions in much the same way as any other employer could be brought to the bargaining table by a national group of unions?

The early initiatives came from America. A majority of the largest multi-nationals had their origins in the United States and America was a massive exporter of capital. So it was not surprising that American unions should be the first to act against a possible drain of jobs abroad. They did so by supporting restrictive trade legislation, but also by trying to put new life into the international trade union secretariats, mostly based in Geneva, which linked unions with members in different countries, but in the same industries—engineering, transport, food, chemicals. The secretariats set themselves broadly similar programmes: to undertake research and the circulation of information; to arrange mutual assistance on an *ad hoc* basis; to co-ordinate the timing of collective bargaining by member unions in national units of multi-nationals around the world; and finally, to engage in genuine collective bargaining across frontiers.

The practical results so far have been slight, though the pace of activity is increasing fast. But so far there have been no real trans-national deals, and the results of *ad hoc* interventions have been meagre. It may be that the chief role of the multi-national in labour relations until now has been as a transmitter of ideas and techniques from one country to another. Thus many unions in Britain took up productivity bargaining in the middle-1960s, a concept which had been introduced into the country by way of the Esso oil company, which had been inspired to try to improve the output of its own employees after making comparisons between its own productivity performance and that of other subsidiaries of its American parent, Standard Oil.

It is much the same story at the European level. There, too, unions have set up trade secretariats to link up unions in the same industries in different member countries of the Common Market.

Relations have been established with some multi-national companies like Philips and Continental Can, but for purposes of consultation only, not collective bargaining. There have been cases of joint action, as when workers in Germany, the Netherlands and Belgium co-ordinated strikes and a factory occupation in 1972 and compelled the chemical company AKZO to re-think plans for closures that would have put 6,000 men from all three countries out of work. Within the Common Market, the nearest to a collective bargain was a 1968 agreement between agricultural union and employer organisations to aim at harmonising the weekly hours of some categories of farmworker. So far as the Common Market itself is concerned, the unions' greatest, and almost their only, success has been to persuade the Brussels Commission to accept their collective view that a version of the German system of co-determination should be included in the statutes for the proposed European company, so that workers would for the first time find places on the boards of transnational companies.

Union internationalism, however, remains in a tentative state. Clearly, going international is one possible future option for the European movement. But there are many obstacles to their doing so. Politics alone will make it difficult. The most powerful unions in France and Italy are communist dominated; those in Germany and Britain are not; they therefore do not belong to the same international organisations and they rarely meet to discuss common programmes and policies. In any case unions are still firmly locked into their own national economic, social and political systems, of which they are themselves the unmistakable products; few things are more characteristically British or French or German than their trade unions. The pace at which the unions internationalise will depend on the pace at which they see the centres of decision that crucially affect their members move outside their own countries —on the speed at which power shifts from Bonn or Rome to Brussels and truly European companies emerge. The advent of Britain to the EEC in 1973 brought the largest single union movement in Europe firmly on to the continental stage and, since the TUC dislikes political bans, this made it more likely that communist and Christian unions would one day be admitted to the European union federation. And the new emphasis given to social questions by the summit meeting of European political leaders in Paris in the autumn of 1972 quickened union interest in the Common Market once more. But whether that interest would be sustained depended on the still doubtful political development of Europe.

The problems of incomes policy were also beginning to take on new shapes in the 1970s. Earlier versions of these policies had been comparatively limited in their scope. Unions were asked—or bribed or cajoled—not to use their full strength in a fully employed labour market to gouge every last penny they could from the employers. Similar restraints were required from other groups, by means of policies to limit price increases and the growth of incomes from sources other than wages and salaries. In so far as they succeeded, policies of this kind had the effect of petrifying incomes in roughly their existing patterns—though at a lower monetary level than they might otherwise have been—but not of disturbing the pattern of incomes itself.

To the unions, especially in countries like Britain and the Netherlands where new versions of incomes policy had been tried time after time, this had come to seem inadequate. If policy had failed to change the distribution of incomes, it had certainly created a far greater awareness of the distribution as it was; and that awareness was increasingly being turned by the unions into a questioning of the status quo. Furthermore, governments were manifestly anxious to enlist the unions' support, for without at least a minimum of this no incomes policy could hope to work. Thus, just as the unions were learning to ask questions, governments were becoming ready to give them the answers they wanted.

So, at the end of 1972, the Dutch unions were able to propose a deal under which, in return for minor or even neutral (in real terms) wage increases, to be distributed equally among all workers in the same industry, the government would agree to step up spending on pensions, education and housing. And in Britain at the same time, the government rounded off a chain of policy reversals aimed at meeting union grievances with a proposal that all wage and salary rises for a twelve-month period should have the same maximum—£2—in order to engage the unions' egalitarian sympathies and win their general support. In the Netherlands, the unions were in effect demanding a voice in the political direction of the economy, and in Britain the government was explicitly offering the unions an economic partnership. However uneasy these overtures were—and in Britain the unions rejected the government's offer completely—they surely marked new beginnings. For it seemed unlikely that future governments would be less eager for union support, or that the unions would be unable to ask an even higher price for giving it.

The unions have many problems left to solve. They must determine their priorities between for instance, equality and incentives; they must resolve their internal dissensions—political and structural, national and international—if they are effectively to represent their members; they must renew and revitalise their own organisations, often far too weak to take advantage of the changed environment—incompetent to meet government or industry on its own ground and unresponsive to the developing needs and wishes of their own memberships.

But if they are capable of grasping their opportunities, the last quarter of the century will see a major expansion of their influence at every level: in Brussels in the multi-national companies, with national governments, in the boardrooms on the shop-floor. This will not be the product of ideology, but of experience; ideologues are far more likely to delay than to advance the unions' progress. Events have written the unions' agenda for them. The equality of the immediate postwar years dissolved with prosperity, but the confidence which workers and their unions acquired from continuous full employment and the new power this gave them over employers and governments has led them to seek a new economic emancipation, to match the political emancipation of universal suffrage. In the early 1970s there was more dissension than peace, more argument than agreement, but the outline of the unions' programme was there to be seen.

Short Bibliography

The principal references and sources are listed at the end of each chapter. This is a brief summary of the sources that have been particularly useful throughout the book.

Industrial Relations in the Common Market, Campbell Balfour, Routledge and Kegan Paul, London, 1972.
Employment Conditions in Europe, Margaret Stewart, Gower Economic Publications, London, 1972.
Wages and Employment in the EEC, Dewi Davies Jones, Kogan Page, London, 1973.
Labour Relations and Employment Conditions in the EEC, Coventry and District Engineering Employers' Association, Coventry, 1972.
Unions in Europe, Eli Marx and Walter Kendall, Centre for Contemporary Studies, University of Sussex, Brighton, 1972.
The Trade Union Movement in the European Community, European Studies, Trade Union Series, The Commission of the European Communities, Brussels 1972.
Some Aspects of Workers' Participation, Christer Asplund, International Confederation of Free Trade Unions, Brussels, 1972.
Inflation: The Present Problem. Report by the Secretary General of OECD, OECD, December 1970.
Present Policies Against Inflation, Report by the Working Party No. 4 of the Economic Policy Committee, OECD, June 1971.
Regional Joint Seminar on Prospects for Labour/Management Co-operation in the Enterprise (papers), OECD, 1972.
Recent Trends in Collective Bargaining, OECD Seminar, Final Report and Supplement, OECD, 1972.

Index